Crab & Winkle

Also by Laurie Duggan

Poetry

East: Poems 1970–74 (1976)
Under the Weather (1978)
Adventures in Paradise (1982, 1991)
The Great Divide, Poems 1973–83 (1985)
The Ash Range (1987; 2nd edition, 2005)
The Epigrams of Martial (1989)
Blue Notes (1990)
The Home Paddock (1991)
Memorials (1996)
New and Selected Poems, 1971–1993 (1996)
Mangroves (2003)
Compared to What: Selected Poems 1971–2003 (2005)
The Passenger (2006)

Cultural history

Ghost Nation (2001)

Crab & Winkle

East Kent & Elsewhere
2006–2007

LAURIE DUGGAN

Shearsman Books
Exeter

First published in the United Kingdom in 2009 by
Shearsman Books
58 Velwell Road
Exeter EX4 4LD

http://www.shearsman.com/

ISBN 978-1-84861-049-1
First Edition

Acknowledgement
This project has been assisted by the Australian Government through the Australia
Council, its arts funding and advisory body.

Australian Government

This long poem contains many quotations, some identified, some not. Some are
from anonymous sources, various technical instructions, Berlin wall graffiti, the
Faversham History website, advertisements, legal documents, newspaper and radio
items, the voices of various pub inhabitants and an audio recording of myself aged
five. Others are from specific individuals, some long dead, some very much alive,
some fictional.

Sections of the work in draft form have appeared in *Jacket*, *onedit* and *The Best
Australian Poems 2008* (Black Inc.). Thanks to the editors of these publications.

I'd especially like to thank Michele Leggott and the New Zealand Electronic Poetry
Centre. A first draft of the opening sections appears online in their Tapa Notebook
series. Thanks also to Larry Stillman for lexicographical advice. And thanks to early
readers of this work especially Lee Harwood, Murray Edmond, Greg O'Brien,
Jenny Bornholdt, Basil & Martha King, Pam Brown, Ken Bolton and
Rosemary Hunter.

This poem was written on a two-year Australia Council Writer's Fellowship (for
2006–2008). My thanks to the Council for their invaluable assistance at a timely
moment.

Crab & Winkle

Prologue

Through cumulus, the hump of Thanet, then Pegwell Bay.

The University of Kent, Canterbury downhill like a 19th century painting, Cathedral dominant. A low-rise city in the valley of the Stour.

A half-timbered hall: Beverley Farmhouse.

A bed that barely fits its room.

September

gathering swallows &c

a rabbit crushed on the road is removed within hours

mown paths
words for angled brickwork?

to dive in amidst all this difference

§

  mushrooms, spongy underside, meaty consistency,
  found in Church Wood near Blean, a warm mid-afternoon

  today 80°, September's hottest recorded?

§

stillness, at 6 pm,
as though readying a season

I sit in the Gulbenkian
(the nearest boozer)

the numeral 19 amid
the verdure

   (large spaces,
plinths with hewn objects
mimicked by insignias on bins,
neat trees

    the 1960s
thought this the closest

architecture came to paradise

no gargoyles to mock aspiration

HIGH VOLTAGE
                    a man
struck by lightning (*timor mortis
conturbat me*) on the side
of a generator

the air thick with smoke

§

compost (this notebook)

vapour trails

it's a pleasure to sit in the slight cool
viewing the campus

a province (so close to London),
the land of Soft Machine and Caravan

§

I have to do battle with Ron Silliman's notion of 'music': that this makes
him seem not so unlike that same School of Quietude he denigrates.
'Music': shouldn't it take care of itself? And the American sense of
'expertise'? We are all inspired amateurs around here.

§

rumori, thunder clouds over the campus
(these move rapidly north-east)

a sense of rain

lighten up
(or tighten up—
Archie Bell & the Drells (or
loosen up—
The Nazz—
or the Alan Bown Set (a
different 'loosen up'

        (O'Hara understood
the importance of all this: a version
of flaneurie
        with a misplaced accent
(mine? here?)
        (*Get the picture?*
Yes, we see.

§

everything at ground level seems quite still

the language of trucks
en route from the tunnel

and news from Australia: the image
of Sasha, Denis and others
in pyjamas, reading books

timor mortis . . .

Sasha's enthusiasms
(how could he *write*, an act
of solitude?)
        Harry Hooton,
a bad poet, but one he cared about
—enough to see the work in print again

O'Hara would have written him up
had he had an O'Hara

                    I remember him
disrobing to white underpants
(a piece on Percy Grainger),

later, walking, with aid
of a stick

                    §

          model aeroplanes in mist
          over the White Horse

          the poets gather
          at the Dark Barn

          (Rudford, Gloucestershire)

          . . . outside the Barn
          a monument to the Welsh
          killed in 1643

          —Gloucester stone

                    §

I can't wrap my mind round the book I'm supposed to review. My lamp,
tested for electrical safety, is no use now (in broad daylight)
                              I rage in a
white *room at* an institutionally coloured
desk

          unaccountably, the memory
          of Kathy Kirby singing
          'Secret Love' and 'Dance On'
          from 1964.

                    §

The road signs don't always work (lost between Ash and Meopham, having missed the A2). Each village signposts only the next.

The couple on the London train—brought together by an introduction agency? Comfortably middle-class, nervously drinking beer on their way to a blues concert. They seemed patently ill-matched though unaware of this, filling each other in with their histories. He was obviously on the make and lacked a degree of self-awareness. She was quite possibly alcoholic, not wishing for sexual intimacy but not wanting to be alone.

On Radio 4 this morning, a debate between the presenter and a radical Muslim from London who keeps using the strange metaphor: *Wake up and smell the coffee!*

§

St Dunstan's: A corner of the cemetery reserved for small children. One grave features a black marble teddy-bear with the photo of a baby on its belly. Next to it, a parrot with wings rotated by the breeze.

the cathedral in the hollow; the army base on the opposite hill.

the light behind the trees
of, was it, Samuel Palmer
signalling an end to something,
the season, or more portentous . . .
late September the fruit
still falling

footsteps in the courtyard
the rattle of leaves on the path

       those spade-like leaves
       are they alder? (the fruit above
       like candles)

the gents stride back to the Registrar's
carrying the kind of cases that ought to contain
                    bundles of bank notes

Hürlimann / Braukunst seit 1836

The spread of architecture as landscape reacts against Piranesian
          compression;
it assumes 'breathing space'.

§

I have functioned as though things put together stood for something, or
rather become something other than what they were before.

the disjuncts are too great . . .

o.k. so Pound said *mind is shapely*
—my mind? I wonder.

elusive bar talk
always seems more than the sum of its parts

a woman picks several leaves of the Alder(?) for
what purpose?—and one decays, blown in,
at the base of a table

(there's no place in a writing school for a poetic predicated on doubt)

our 'worldly goods' somewhere in the Indian Ocean

§

                a man
                a map
                amen

§

a huge black & white cat crosses the plaza
& climbs the grassy verge of the library

a curved corrugated roof
begins to merge with the sky.

what's out there will always exceed art

rab éfac / amenic / ertaeht

remembering that line of The Angelic Upstarts:
I want two pints of lager and a packet of crisps please

§

back to the old drafts of a poem that
has lost its way

         the sky darkens
and everything seems quite still

across the road a fortnight ago
the bus shelter was stripped of flyers
and painted brown
         a week later
it was bulldozed.
         an orange spotlight
directed at this building is often turned off
at night
       this is the season
for mosquitoes

a pattern: the sky clears late afternoon

§

In Oxford: the Ashmolean

Tintoretto's resurrection
Piero di Cosimo—animals fleeing a fire
an anon (?) work showing a French siege, where the armoured figures
          inhabit flattened perspective like Wyndham Lewis
Uccello—the Hunt
Sickert's 'Ennui'
the sculpted head of Lorenzo di Medici
a watercolour by Natalia Goncharova
some old men in a work by, was it, Veronese?

October

cloudbursts passing over
(last night, thunder)

time to read about the 'poetry wars'

late afternoon the sky opens up
—I mean, lightens—the city below
revealed clearly, its outlying power lines
the military base diagonally opposite

§

how, by an almost complete avoidance
the matter of . . .
                         those who would spell it out
lose out

the matter of England?
the shadow of a football spinning from a knee,
Spitfire Ale (how Kentish)

§

What would youth be like? I mean how ironic are they, who look just
like I looked, are full, undeniably, of the same self-importance (mine, I
suspect, the more naïve)? I would love that sense of centrality, of things
being within my reach. They're not, of course. Though no further away
than from them, probably. (*Notionally* . . . thanks Ken). Anyway, I wish
them well. It's a harder place than it was.

§

harvest moon (due tomorrow,
possibly obscured by clouds)

the prisons overflowing
—why don't they resume transportation
or moor hulks in the Thames?

(they do)

§

my scrawl
my screed

getting to the point
(or getting to the pint)?

'brewed since 1698'
—a decade after the 'glorious revolution'

§

drive through the rain
to Whitstable to eat vegan
(in my leather jacket)

suddenly moss is noticeable, in a pocket
on the south-east of this building—
it must have been there all along?

I reach for books
that aren't yet here

(the harvest moon, full nearest
autumn solstice, would be large
on the horizon were it visible)

In the morning paper: Britain really is a shrinking island (erosion).

§

the head of George Barker
upside down on a bookshelf

the stars   (a telescope)
& electric guitars

the revised
solar system

the smiling face of
a telephone on wheels

an inverted funnel
on the head of a hippopotamus

all the bears, frogs and pandas
are asleep

somewhere in Cambridge

§

dismember last year's poem ('One-Way Ticket')
into small pieces
                    & date however

the mizzle lifts from Faversham

At Oare Marshes the coast is thick with bird-watchers (tripods and
telephoto lenses). The road peters out at Harty Ferry; tracks rise from
the water on Sheppey, the other side.

§

a site
for sore eyes   (this apartment)
its grimy carpets

rising damp
a state of life

(not 'a floor you could eat off', a floor
many people have eaten off

here, in territory
described by a Londoner in Wellington NZ
as *blooody tropical*

§

convergence
at equinox
                    the hiss
of remote cars
                    a spot
of rain

            imagining interiors
a house, circa 1750
in West St

        subject to
movement and associated distortion
over the ensuing period

§

1750—the date of Piranesi's *Fanciful images of Prisons, etchings published by Buzard in Rome, conducting business on the Corso.*

§

the rabbits have disappeared

(the big ampersand)
a plug-in infinity

the shadow of a creature
on the upper branches

(gaps in the foliage)

inside:
our minimal décor

notebooks, sheets
on which a poem dismantles

a large spider emptied into the garden

§

Could 'One-Way Ticket' work as a small book, the gaps as sections or
page breaks?

It does!

§

greyness, and why
a handful of leaves
alone should have coloured

a backward text
erupts through this one

maps show the way to markets
a scale you could step into

where to obtain these portions
these well-lit cover photographs

as Hardy's soil throws darkness
back at the sky

a notice-board pieces our life together
as debt and adventure

the windows (begrimed casements)
impossible to clean

and now, a light from the street
visible through shifting foliage
an almost-silence, mid-weekend
(the denizens elsewhere)

illness is a kind of boredom
—like *money is a kind of poetry*

      intelligible?
      illegible?

      the king's reall or his
      stamped face?

      outlines of squirrels in the branches
      like 1930s woodcuts by Eric Ravilious

§

In the *Guardian* an item on bushfires & drought in south-east Australia.
Another season's stock lost. The Darling River almost dry. So much is
still 'up in the air'. Our possible residence a tangle of legalities. We have
the contents of four suitcases plus a small pile of books.

§

these glum bedsits
bred psychedelia

       though the English
in their songs were always
home for tea

(blotting paper with chips?)
           or
mother . . . I'm in a field
somewhere in England
and I've lost part of my brain
           (Jarvis Cocker)

children's books were the oddest things
to fall back on
       a hatch
in the back of a wardrobe
         (a way out
of the Home Counties

§

    extended summer period: the hottest since
    1629 (?)
        66° in London at 6pm.

Universities to 'monitor' Islamic students' activities

The forecast today is 'rain', but Kent seems to defy prediction. The 'weather' happens elsewhere—or simply, this microclimate isn't recorded by Radio 4 (last night: in the station parking lot listening to a program about hedgehogs, frost on the car windows).

§

I can't read your poems, I suffer from Silliman's Ear

§

this farmhouse like a ship, beached
on a hillside in Kent (& these rooms
with all the disadvantages of ships' cabins)

the large window faces north-west, a court
of decaying cardboard boxes, assorted junk,
a laundromat
                the smaller one, south-east,
the university grounds and the forest, strewn
with food cartons and disposables
                        on either side
constant human traffic
                  inside, Elizabethan
beams, 1970s dormitory doors with faux-medieval handles, fire notices,
peeling paintwork, boot-sale furniture

a cracked mirror

timetables, council tax bills, various regional maps

an enormous fireplace

§

I realise that in this English university setting I expect to see British actors
as dysfunctional academics, but instead I get British academics who
appear (slightly) like actors.

il pleut doucement sur la ville

Some years ago P's goods (from Australia) arrived at the Liverpool docks
in time for a waterside workers' strike. He lived out of a suitcase for
eight months.

Where is the lightning bolt? The implausible John Martin landscape? As they say in the badly-translated futurist movie: 'Romanticism! You are finished!'

§

(night)
diagonals of rain
earlier—the English
taking the sunlight while it lasts

(though this season has been
overly long).

I do not miss my country

squirrels nibble the damp course

& there is nothing
upon the long mantelpiece

(on the floor:
Not Everything Remotely;
Understanding Property)

§

Poetry is a kind of ecological practice. You want things to be around (maybe not in 3 point something million years when the Milky Way collides with some other gaseous body, but for a while at least, where time makes sense. Does my desire for this render me an outcast? Or just a not-so-ideal specimen of homo economicus?

§

two strawberries in Pewsey on
October the 11th 1906

a jar of Kentish mustard

scuds of rain
a collapsed umbrella

§

a maintenance man came hammering
                    hammering
                    hammering

                              just as the upstairs inhabitants
seem to shift furniture at 3 am
—maybe they're making a bomb?

whom bomb?

& the overweight guy
who steps outside the door every 15 minutes to smoke.

is that precipitation
or just a fine coat of dirt?

there's no spectacular 'turn' so far
just dead leaves
                    the laundry's done at least

§

(those back room figures in Velázquez' early paintings
—a sketchy Christ viewed through an opening—
as they wash bowls, prepare dishes
all of them looking much like the inhabitants
of Seville circa 1620.

The sad post-coital Mars, a testament
to middle-age

Outside in the wet, Covent Garden, waiting for a train.

And the day before that sheltered by cliffs at St Margaret's, the Channel walled by container vessels.

And the day before that, a movie that my lack of narrative sense transformed into a raft of inconsistencies. I mean I hadn't worked out who was telling the story and someone's character changed unaccountably ('Why I am not a movie critic').

§

the promise of a cold morning
this record I keep
                      Pam en route for Melbourne;
the oddness of departure: the way a habitation
becomes other, once packed; a space, once
of personality, something we'd think
hard to leave, gone, already
from memory.
                  & how many years yet
for Ken & Cath, in Adelaide?

it's not a virtue of mine to be *no trouble*,
perhaps an inadequacy.

                  a fire-alarm test
faults us badly, failing to take account
of a certain weariness, dealing with a situation
as contrived as this.

my friends in their various places, I think of you all
(hoping that Jenny is well in Wellington)

as I await the frost

(the fire alarm labelled: 'Bardic #5')

§

Some change in the form of life, gives from time to time a new epocha of existence.
In a new place there is something new to be done, and a different system of
thoughts rises in the mind. I wish I could gather currants in your garden.

—Dr Johnson

§

increasingly dark afternoon
though 'good news'
 (= MONEY)
in the post

buy more books!

                    it's feeling,
say the weather people, more like November.

the prognosis for the planet is not good

transcribe notes
in the office up the hill
                    (I can't read
                    my own writing)

§

          of John Anderson,
his deep ecology
                    the thought of it now
buried in three small books in a container
'somewhere in England'.
                    a respite here
from the deluge, banks of cloud, moving
quickly, this room floored with sunlight

& this, in praise of the lost poets

(the publishers
were not in love with his diagrams
—seemingly crude maps
of connectedness

now the effect
of all things
only too apparent

bands of sunlight
on that chair, the map
of Canterbury crossed by shadow

aeration
& waiting

§

Dr Johnson: *If I had no duties, and no reference to futurity, I would spend my*
life in driving briskly in a post-chaise with a pretty woman [cars & girls 1777?]

§

the Stour and its tributary channels
gush about Deans Mill
and under St Radigund's

a network of one-ways
it seems impossible to navigate

—other end of town, the old tannery
up for development, as back lanes
connect old pubs and uncertain sites

after a day of sunlight the grey blanket
comes down and everything stills

§

The Barbican
The Hayward Gallery
Tate Modern (for drinks only)

Josef Sudek: the detritus of lunch; condensation on a window

Stanislaw Witkiewicz: the self as multiple personality; the look outlasting
the looker

Henryk Ross: a scaffold; a melting negative

Jikka Hanzlová: the tint of grass-blades; luminous tree trunks

    make something
    out of eggshells
    shadows of
    passers-by

    the long hook
    hanging from a cross-
    beam

    dance of light
    on a toast-rack

pipes with their ornate brackets, out
from the gutterings
a tradesman's clatter
opening two doors

nail holes
in the wall

§

the consequences of our inaction
will be irreversible

§

   Rye:
a former port, beached (or beachless)—a hill
in the levels, where every second shop
sells 'antiques'.

a woman carries a jug of beer up the street

distant shapes of the nuclear plant (across Romney
Marsh).

§

The train to Margate is a myth. Monitors show different times. People just sit on the platform patiently (in an icy wind). I get a refund and go to the 'Goods Shed' for coffee (the market). It's 45 minutes since 'breakfast' and 45 before 'lunch'.

The sense of a different time-frame. In 1992 when we spent three months in Britain it felt like an age. We've been here now two months: in one sense it seems not so long at all, yet in another sense a great deal seems to have happened. We lived (1992) from suitcases. But I had plastered a wall of student residence with postcards and magazine cuttings (there seemed to be more art in 'Arts' magazines back then). I kept a proper diary, a page at least of description every day.

. . . . but this is:

half-diary, half-what?   *The opening of the*
field?

(half-man, half-diary)

the lamp's angle reveals brush strokes on plasterboard
a great sea of institutional off-white
the odd dip and puttied hole

a Freudian ship

in which we serve

November

fire alarm at lunch
dishes at empty tables, but only a few
re-enter the building. I prefer this icy wind
to dullness and showers . . .

THERE IS AN [   ] INTERVAL

. . . and yet there are
midriffs here, unaware as Goths in Miami

the view of the city is as clear (possibly) as
it gets

subtropical plants
upstairs in the octagon

new courses in complexity science

THERE IS [   ] NO INTERVAL

§

in Sudek's Prague
condensation on windows
the running lines reveal a fruit tree in the yard
—tonight frost is rumoured
in memory of those small areas of humidity
where objects cast their shadows
and the sky, a uniform grey
is broken by damp glass

here, closer to the sea
& the north wind, rime
on car windows held, for the moment . . .

red wine in a panelled room,
noodles, stirred, in a pot

the blocks, morphing
from brick to wood,
worm-holes, marks of borers
in greying texture,
charcoal zigzag
up the rear wall of the hearth
beneath the bressummer

a tarnished mirror

what does not change / is the will to change

§

days of obituaries

the self, fading
into sepia

the accidents
of cooking

vita brevis

the month
a mouth

alarums!
electronic sounds
outside

art is long
and life is
breakfast

§

Margate. The remnants of Gormley's burnt figure on the lot, Dreamland.

ICE COLD BEER SERVED IN PLASTIC GLASSES

The rest of it—the amusement park, a tarmac stacked with objects, large
waste bales that seem to construct dwellings.

coffee at the Harbour Café-Bar, the north wind shut out.
a van arrives with eggs, steam
on the windows, the Promenade blocking the sea front

decaying palaces of the upper classes

                                   the prow of Thanet
cut off by cheap flights
                        the Isle unmoored.

who was Dane John? his gardens, sunlit,
in the midst of all this ruin?
                              apartments
named after ships (Nelsons?) steer into
a bluff northerly.
                    on the station:
Welcome to Dreamland, posters for a 'tea dance'
(one half expects Vera Lynn to make a guest appearance)

§

remember those who cared about poetry
(as the light dims inadvertently in the bar):
Shelton Lea, once 'dangerous'
in a blue suit; latterly
walking with a stick, a *dandy in the underworld*
whose love for the craft was undiminished
—what place for Shelton in *this* world?

the romantics were fucked, but try telling *him*.
he could have stepped back and conversed
with Dr Johnson, this lost heir
to confectionery fortunes.

                  Alan Wearne
had a nose for the real ones
who'd fit in no survey,
even ΠO, public service anarchist
who wrote better than anyone: a Greek
taking notes from a Turk (Nâzim Hikmet)

interrupting my reverie, French lovers on the sofa adjoining, hum of the
bar

what of the pace of art, in a place
where darkness takes over the season?
(sudden applause from the 'drinks' end of the bar)
did the artists 'struggle' for light (more applause),
'chasing' it, for example
in St Ives?

§

MUSGRAVE. *'A temporary poem always entertains us.'*
JOHNSON. *'So does an account of the criminals hanged yesterday entertain us.'*

§

logics appear when *the world is
everything that is the case*

all these notebooks, these unanticipated
corners, a map
blown-up, fresh detail inserted

the removal of that rail line
—the Crab and Winkle Way—a path
over the hill to Whitstable . . .

the grand projects become miscellanies

my greatest skill: the ability to 'waste time'

§

How would I identify those ragged bushes round the farmhouse wall?
Leaves paired from the stem a leaf-width gap between shoots (say three
centimetres)?

§

> fireworks
> would not have happened
> in the war
>> *the coast of Kent lit up*

fields of spent rockets

(fields of rocket colonised the London bombsites
did anyone eat it?
or was it just an unwanted plant
in unoccupied space?)

Fireworks seem to fit the season—unlike Australia—since all this display
coincides with dying light. Fawkes, the pretext for an older concern.

§

> Holbein at Tate Britain: matter
> and people who matter
> (the texture of those garments which,
> a century later, would become less substantial
> —style, or heating?

down Regent Street to Piccadilly Circus
in search of warm clothes. the day

starting to close in now
around three

          (light dimming already
through the one window of
the Turner rooms. He sought it
(Turner, light): those 1840 paintings
their skeins (skins) thin and infinite

              (A proposed Turner gallery,
Margate, abandoned—it was out on a pier—presumably for reasons
of insurance and escalation of building costs in an era where such a
structure would rapidly become unfeasible: the rock of Thanet itself
safe (probably), though submerged partially by ice-melt. By 2050, *the east
coast of England washed away by tsunami.*

Turner strapped to the mast

§

the adjacent room consumed by a fireplace
usable only as a shelf for wet shoes

and *this* room, its desk
upon which I cannot write

(but I am writing it)
              in grey light
at 2.30 pm
watching paint dry
(the wall; Turner's Thanet Coast)
gummed squares that held the image of something

§

Ross Gibson on the *location* (& locution) of Ed Kuepper's 'Electrical Storm':
that sense of lying, glued to the linoleum floor, waiting for any kind of
relief . . .

but I have climbed out
of Brisbane's climate and into
a box of words; I live
amid documents

—and Kuepper's 'Storm' is one of these—

on the table: *The English Legal System* (8th
edition ed. Slapper & Kelly)

the air itself
anticipates decay

contracts / documents of ownership
their responsibilities
a legal trail
muddied from the 70s as Council writ

—the closer something gets the further away it seems;
the possibility of it being snatched or
rendered inaccessible

to read
or not to read
'the fine print'

§

leaf mould

dusk at Chartham, smoke
from burning bracken

The other morning in the supermarket two men behind me in the queue
sounded like they were doing Wallace & Gromit impersonations—but it
was their real voices.

Last night the frost took some clearing from the windscreen. We ate old-style Italian in Whitstable & the maître d' showed us marks on the wall from the 1954 flood; the whole of the town (as it was then) submerged, almost.

§

That Ed Dorn and Jonathan Williams both passed through Black Mountain College says a lot for the institution (I think this while reading Gavin Selerie's *Azimuth*).

A dark barn and laughter issuing forth

first Pound's cosmology, then Olson's (geography subsumes history)
and then the collapse of systems,
the translation of text into footnote
                              (Dorn's *La Jolla, Abhorrences*)

(praise to W.C. Williams
for writing out of the possibility of not writing
or writing out that possibility
(*The Descent of Winter*)

                    all of this lost
on fans of the 'writing school' Williams.
I think of his anger *that good doctor*
(from which *Paterson* even
was a falling off, though a fine one)
the reclamation of an older
more surreal America, its pure products
crazier now than ever

§

to place a marble slab, just so
uphill, behind the residence

polarised light, ponds in mud
on the glass, some trees
leafless almost, others
yet to turn

in the mail: voices, an invoice
from Exeter
                    (my uncle-in-law's steam-train visits to cathedral cities
is the world I'm part of, yet no expert on
—an export, not an expert)
                                        what
of what we write
would survive, dug up as fragments?

§

Trees with the density of a Gainsborough uphill over the roof of the
laundry. A bruised sky behind a dead branch.

mellow mists and fruitfulness

the air perhaps, of a John Everett Millais painting
as in light through casements the texture
of materials—soft wool—the overall sense
of decay and beauty—that high Victorian
back-to-back
                    the lovers' seat
                    the death seat

and *this* room, a drying cupboard

§

                    them down there
                    rolling in
                    their beautiful vowels

namers of things and
shapers of thought

§

a man with a blowtorch
fixes the tarred roof of the Tizard building

a tight-
ness in the stomach,

a wish for before and after to merge
(no present)

do things settle
too easily, become
the prospect from a window?

no spontaneous drawing
                            these records
assembled from nothing much
for what future?

my needs, mostly padding of sorts,
a place from which to function

§

The thought of diligent people working on our complete destruction:
the projects (official and unofficial) of the new world.

I feel, in a cosmological sense, like one of those, carrying a blackboard on
my back, seen in an Iranian movie—the bearer of displaced 'expertise'

though I sense we have all become 'migrants'.

§

a bird, greenish, with long tail:
a woodpecker?
                              elusive out on the lawn
—except that woodpeckers don't have long tails,
at least not the large green ones

it's a quiet night at the 'office'—or I'm early
there are courses here in stand-up comedy
                                              some of them
(the students) must be at an adjoining table
                                              'ha ha', or, 'boom boom'

a young man in a suit
with an appalling haircut
(think John Farnham circa 1970)

one with tiny round glasses and wiry hair
like an escaped Marx brother

grace equals guts under pressure
or *guts equals grace under pressure*
but Tom Clark says
                      ('Code of the West')
pleasure is never mentioned.

                              amid this goonery
I should mention it more often

two men, duck walk
carrying a third, stiff as a plank
and bug-eyed (the bar mural)

the world is everything that is the case

including those earnest 'others'
plotting our destruction

I'm, I guess, a diasporic figure (diasporic for several generations) but the
point of diaspora is that there is no longer a 'homeland', there is no place
where we 'belong'.

white shapes of crockery
stacked above the Gaggia
as staff polish the equipment
(work perceived—as important
as work done—in the new economy).

this is my 'Flash', my 'Baci', for the moment.
and is ΠO, this very moment drinking coffee in Fitzroy?
and Pam and Jane in Elwood, a further stage in *their* peripatetic life?

§

crowns, branches
now visible
in the trees,
and cars in the carpark

§

In London Gavin and Frances, their traces, and John Seed who said
Sheerness (Isle of Sheppey) was the image of a 1950s working-class
town. I imagined the Prince of Wales ordaining this but it was no parody
and grim enough.

employment in manufacturing has slumped to its lowest level since 1841

§

                              gusts
gather about the farmhouse
                              we wait on details
for the move to Faversham
                              legalities
for the compleat adult
                         often blundered through
(those administering them
no better prepared)
                         the great weight
of English law

                    §

drive to Brighton across the Weald and the South Downs
a blue sky's feathered jetstreams

walk downhill to the beach
the burnt out shape of the old pier
& the heritage-coloured front

photos of Lee's ancestors in New Zealand
—the South Island, out of Christchurch;
wagons pulled by a steam tractor
(this one used for the cover of *Landscapes*)

a truly weird book (something about Bulgaria and Henrik Ibsen, super-hero)
by Jocelyn Brooke, its illustrations
like a native Max Ernst; Brooke's book on orchids
in which the illustrator dates his images, slightly foxed

                    §

half a century of animal skins in America
and the Astors came back rich
to Hever Castle, to Eton and Margaret Thatcher
—forced to sell out in 1982

(the elder Astor's faux Tudor additions from 1905)
this former residence of Anne Boleyn (Bullen)
just off the M25.

                               Waxworks in the Long Hall
cut Henry VIII down to size—or from size:
he was 6 ft tall *and* beefy, quite prepared
to do the work of a mafia grandee

                                       the house
passing (in between) to Catholics who hid a chapel
behind a bedroom.

                             Astor put his children in the attic
after the floods of 1968

                    §

walking through
imaginary interiors
modes of being amid
what furniture?

                  my garb?
                  myself?

removing dead leaves and mud
from carpets

                  the rich in their
                  handsome panelling
                  somehow penurious
—everything (Hever) too big
or too small
                  in which to exhibit the self

(how easy it was for the Astors
to insert their selves into verities
like robber barons centuries previous)

                  the cargo of the 'Sirius'
                  could have been decided
                  by lottery

§

at Whitstable, the pub on the beach, almost washed
away 50 years back. floor sagging as a ship's deck;
the memory of a dart board
                        along the front
not all the double-glazing *will keep out*
the Lord's burning rain
                        at least that personage's ocean,
Southend on the horizon.
                        I buy a black jumper,
wool and alpaca, then drive back, over the rise
to Canterbury.

a coppice, up the hill, in half-light

the youth of England, furtive
in a car park, up to
some obvious illegality

§

Henry VIII is not so remote. The poisoners
and political procurers are still with us. It feels
like Rome in its decline

                    hovering, marginal
in the face of immense disregard

                the Mandelsons, their kind, elevated
                devoid of shame: death
                on a large scale elsewhere.
                                    to bear witness:
                Steve Bell, his cartoons, more vicious
                than any Australian could imagine:
                Bush and Blair dog paddle in a cistern

§

a quietness
too late   too early

confined in these rooms, to imagine more than this

distant sirens   a car door
somewhere closer,

a train leaves Canterbury West

§

turnstones
picking at the rocks
Whitstable beach

(a winter bird)

§

through Chartham the wet descends,
bare poplars, the hedges thinning,
a black Rolls-Royce on a muddy track

the entire landscape
steam on a window

railyards, late November
acres of mud cling to treads,
digging vehicles, detritus
broken concrete, unused piping
a whole field of neon tubes lit up as candles

a field of geese out of Tonbridge

§

in the Miller's Arms: Christmas lights, a fire,
looking out over the canal. Spitfire at room temperature
(spitfires at three o'clock sir!)
                              ivy shows up
on the trunks and last year's pollarding,
the parasites still green,
above the canal, the Doric order in iron.

doors sealed against the wind (or the
traffic)—not much of either at present. a slow
trail of students towards the city.
                              the sound
(on the system) of English folk—modern, not
'finger-in-the-ear'—a brightness
in the season
                    the sun already at such an angle
(does darkness fall *like a wet sponge?*)

the slight pleasure, these hours, of seeing
people, lit, in their kitchens,
oblivious preparations (the kitchen so often
at the front of these buildings).
                              a wall basket
(outside) demonstrates the wind,
not so cold as yet. A woman on the pavement,
smiles to herself.

in the main street the decorations are up

the little bulbs go on and off

INLAND [image] *REVENUE*
APPLICATION for a CERTIFICATE under Section II
(1) of the Finance Act, 1894

§

Avebury, its stones in rain,
hot chocolate, a run to the car through mud

arriving at Bath, peak traffic,
weather coming in up the valley

it's quiet above the crescents & circuses,
Saturday morning, someone at work in their office,
radial treetops, branches against the pale stone, the
stepped Georgians

the man, bent over some charter, natural light
through large windows

                someone on a sill
                in the distance, smoking,
                three floors up

the amber underside of cloud, a blue band, then
rooftops. a stand of trees on the horizon,
wave shaped by winds

a ladder of angels

& Gwen John, her cats
her sketches,
           a Gainsborough, roughly executed

in the abbey, memorials to Arthur Phillip
& Isaac Pitman
             the ruin and rebuilding
             after iconoclasm

At Wells cathedral, mid-morning service: the organ rumbles enough to
tilt the psyche off orbit. The sculpted exterior is as close as Christianity
gets to Hinduism but the size of the edifice is more the product of a power
struggle between Wells and Bath than any indication of spirituality. The

Bishop's immense palace and the parish church at Wells are as large as most cathedrals.

the town, reddish sandstone
c.f. the limestone of Bath.
in the street, children with Somerset accents

The 'levels' were islands joined by wooden bridges. You descend to them from the Mendips, Glastonbury Tor on the horizon.

—I'm reminded, writing this,
of Rexroth, his jaded tour
through postwar Britain
comprising mainly of encounters
with Hooray Henrys and
friendly prostitutes. His regard
for Britain's literary establishment
minimal.
              It was the age of Shell Guides
the celebration of quaintness amid bad cooking
                              though Rexroth himself
seemed a relic when he visited Australia decades later
—a slightly false prophet of the counter-culture,
above it, yet pathetically beholden to it.

theatres take *the shape*
of a moon in its decrease (Alberti)
and hence John Wood's Crescent at Bath;
the moon in this phase
as we walk down the hill Saturday evening
to dine in the town centre

§

A dull country magistrate gave Johnson a long tedious account of his exercising his criminal jurisdiction, the result of which was his having sentenced four convicts to transportation. Johnson, in an agony of impatience to get rid of such a companion, exclaimed, 'I heartily wish, Sir, that I were a fifth.'

—Boswell

§

aquae Sulis
a.k.a. Minerva

viewed from afar
Dvrovernvm

Cathedrals appear from a distance, disappear in the middle ground then loom when you approach them through the streets. The middle distance is the realm of town-planners.

§

a woman picks her way across boggy grass
in high heels

the double sound of a train leaving Canterbury West
and a half-whistled fragment of Eric Satie
(*Eric Satie / sat at tea*)

the needs for a writing
of this kind,
a certain space, and,
not a *derangement of the senses*
but some diffraction occasioned by that space.

late November, almost the end
for the spotted shark (a Torres Strait carving on the calendar).
also on the shelf, the image
of a pair of thongs, Japanese umbrellas,

a card with coloured dots—either this is
a copy of Damien Hirst, or else, possibly,
Damien Hirst copied the card?

§

we escape our own history
to live in someone else's,
navigating National Trust classifications
(that specify the exact green
of a garage door)

> a stoat
> on the gravel path
> possibly a weasel,
> then, last night
> a small black mouse in the flat
> (maybe a shrew?) hid
> under the bed

§

at Chartham, pup tents on the edge of ponds
(bird watching)

a bonfire
in the woods
near Pluckley

(impossible to write
on a moving train)

'Padlock Wood'

the white cones of oast houses

blue / white flowers in the hedges look like frost

'Hitler Green'

Georgian architecture: the beginning of modern space, then Ford Madox Brown's suburbia—how to read it: as monstrous? What was once gimcrack now seems well built.

a trembling man with a palm-pilot
figures dancing under a tree

what place amid textings for an ancient art?

here, now, at The Marquess of *what*?, Covent Garden

I'm unlocatable
'somewhere in London'

December

The Descent of Winter? Possibly.
(the warmest autumn since . . .

no sign of the Royal Mail   (the writing
gets *littler and littler*
                              (a review
finished yesterday, deranged, maybe
—but on deadline
                    (someone outside
in a parka, like the Michelin man
                              (car lights
the excess of energy. Will there be anyone
to remember us?
                    (would Frank O'Hara
enjoy it while it's there
                              (the syntax
strangely wrong
                    (begin again

§

marked on the directory: the Oxo tower
—an advertisement for beef-cubes—
a palindrome at the centre of an empire

At the dining hall of the Inner Temple the consumption of wine has
fallen off since the advent of the internet (letters would formerly be
answered in the morning).

Sir John Soane's museum is a surrealist trouvé,
stones, plaster casts and false walls,

skylights of all shapes, a sarcophagus:
the house designed as a place of instruction

Hogarth ('The Rake's Progress' and 'The Election'),
Turner, Piranesi (the pen and ink sketches, not the more rigid etchings)

portraits of Napoleon,
a Chinese dog,
images of Shakespeare,
fragments, an arm,
parts of a head

(followed by coffee at Somerset House)

§

for the moment
the movement
to solstice,
the radio seems to come on earlier
(odd to be drinking tea in darkness)

§

Martin Johnston remembered here: his parents' months in London, after
which Greece was paradise. But that was 1949 and rationing. Martin, a
year or two older than me, dead in his forties (his family had an appalling
survival rate). Will he be reprinted?

§

buy shoes in Sandwich
                    imagining ourselves
frozen, on the path to the seafront, discovered
two millennia hence: the 'Sandwich People'

Location? On the 'Green Wall' adjacent to the watercourse called 'Vigo

Sprong', before the Saxon Shore Way crosses the Royal St George Golf
Course.

§

Basil King's 'Arc' arrives in the mail. His
testimony continues, an outburst of energy taking in
a history of art, of transgression, of left-handed
pitchers,
            a search for perfect pitch?

—but a sense of Baz, his connection
with De Kooning, with Olson and Creeley
(and the Blitz)
                you understand,
reading him, why an artist must produce,
this intensity, this need,
though the materials may be no more than
a hand, a deck of cards, a beauty spot
(once these were carried in small containers, the
artificial moles of the eighteenth century).
                                    the arc
is the call of crows, the weld of instances
here, on the ground, in Kent, as thinned branches
disclose their populations.
                        monitor this,
testify to this.   well,
I will, in my own way.

§

            artificial light on grass, the trunks
of various trees, that mix of lime green
and black.
            letters to various people.

having to be out among it
parts of the day, despite conditions

(if heat became something else
in John Forbes' poems, could cold
in mine?)

       gentlemen's outfitters
       in which you might buy a deerstalker
       maybe even plus-fours

§

evening: the George, to celebrate
purchase of moleskins, prior to reading
at the Menzies Centre.
              a scarf and a woollen cap
that makes me look like an escapee from an institution.

Mark O'Connor (the one we used to call 'the real'
a.k.a. John Nash, author of *Ode to Iggy Pop*)
once said: *who could feel bad in a hotel?*
Here (England) it makes more sense—the old saw
about Americans going to bars to be alone, the English
for company. It's their living space, away from
poky parlours and bedsits. those chandeliers,
rows of golden taps,
             and: paradise!
they play 'You're gonna miss me'
by the 13th Floor Elevators! Roky Erikson is a genius!

§

     a small tornado in North London
     (blizzards forecast for the new year)
     lasted no more than a minute
           (ten streets affected)
it's just surreal man, I was asleep
      and a rooftop came through my window

§

all colour gone from the courtyard (except
wet green)
            a leaf clinging to the threshold . . .

wheat beer, at the Continental, Whitstable,
buoys rocked on the chill, Southend obscured,
bluster gradually clearing from the S.W.
as waves break over the groyne
                       water flutters
on the surface of a barrel
                 the next room full
of mothers and children: this is an English afternoon.

You realise your own moderation
(the 18th century permanently drunk—Johnson
didn't even regard cider as 'drink', or beer either
probably, though the quantity of port consumed
might mean it wasn't so strong
—how enter that mindset now?
                    And how could they enter ours?
of radiation-poisoned operatives or minute-by-minute
exposés.
        no lengthy talk in coffee-houses
(with my attention span could I do this?)

when jacketed walkers open the back flap
a dog falls out of a car

a smudge on the horizon vanishes.

§

Christmas rush in Canterbury
the main street impossible to move in
(when's St Agnes Eve? it's chill already)

my bad handwriting
where 'Christmas rush'
looks like 'Christmas noh'
(a homage to Murray Edmond?)

—Christmas noh could be interesting e.g.
One: 'I can't move in this street'
Two: 'Why are you here then?'
One: 'Because I need an overcoat'
A man staggers past carrying an enormous sign, the
      lettering of which is illegible.

etcetera

§

rotten apples under trees near Selling
rotten apples on blue carpet
at the V & A museum

The Victorian age, represented by the Albert Memorial, Hyde Park, and
Julia Margaret Cameron's illustration of Tennyson. A deep vulgarity in
both cases though vulgarity and vitality often run together: a four-foot
Queen's mourning and the literalism of Victorian art (this or a vision of
hell: Harrod's Knightsbridge in the Christmas rush).

a writing like weaving where
letters become emblems

§

In nine days this place closes down for winter break. Only the security
guards in their heated vans, possibly no mail . . .

winter hobby: bedraggling

sleep

brother of the unabomber
RADIO 4

§

heading south into the sun at nine-thirty
to the Goods Shed where the surface of the wooden tables
is warm from overhead heating.

a row of unskinned rabbits (or hares?) draining perhaps,
'turkey foil'
               fanlights onto platforms

cabbage steam over the balustrade
(though, here, suitably herbed, perhaps in cider vinegar)

that doubled sense of seasonally appropriate decoration

the wood, soaped, worn smooth, faint rings of coffee.

a few months more of the exotic
then what?

§

chestnuts, bought a week back, emit blue powder.
they're mouldy, I discover, on boiling and shelling.

§

four weeks for the Swale Council to sign a piece of paper
rescuing our books from imprisonment (somewhere in West London)
—and my big overcoat;
our paintings (what space for these
in the new abode?)
numerous forgotten items

it's 3 pm, lighting up time (and still
lunatics in short-sleeved shirts) Hello Ken!
& dear Pam, homeless in Melbourne, as we
are homeless in Canterbury

merryberry Chris-
anthemums to all!

§

bird sounds
tape loops

§

Faversham newsagent's window: *no more than 2 young persons in this shop at*
a time

flagged rear of The Sun (woodbeams not sunbeams)

pheasant fillet £2 ea.

a draught felt faintly
—the sense of how cold seeps in

fucking walking
on broken glass

§

it's getting quieter at the Farmhouse (though still the doors bang at 2 am).
the old notebook typed up (almost), ready to send to New Zealand.

Art. No. 189/46 PP / FINE 0,3

the sky hasn't lifted,
shouting, possibly footballers, up

in the car park,   sagging remnant
of a kite in the upper branches

not the dark but the getting dark

a faint whistle: the heaters? illuminated folders
in someone's office, long silences
broken by people in stairwells

the disappearance of water voles
the continuance of arms trading

§

What stood on the south side of Canterbury where the ring road and
the picture theatre now stand? The whole area around there, the new
shops &c, was it a bomb-site?

§

in Margate (the house
formerly owned by Hattie Jacques and John Le Mesurier
marked with a blue NT plaque.
                              (three floors,
overlooking the sea).
                              down the street, a door
which, whenever open, reveals men
drinking around a low table, Trinity Square
near the Wintergarden.

§

The disappeared: Bill Beard, ex-RAAF beat poet, last seen working as a
fire-watch on the Victorian and NSW borders, avoiding the 'commercial'
world of publishing. He occurs after reading John Welch's account of
'literary' figures in Soho and the London of the 1960s, those who lived
hard for art and who remain, if at all, as footnotes (walk-ons) in other

people's lives. These figures never got so far as 'grub street', some barely published at all, remembered perhaps in someone else's account of a poetry reading in a building that no longer exists.

§

white frost, a view of the Cathedral spires,
smoke plumes: Canterbury, the sun
rising through cloud, 8.30 am.

The computer lab is empty. Every few minutes I have to get up and do a little dance to turn the lights back on.

Pam and Jane, having sold up and moved to Melbourne, now want to move back to Sydney, or rather the Blue Mountains (which are not Sydney). Other than my friends, their news, all I hear of Australia is cricket, drought, and the Australian Wheat Board scandal. In the English papers the place may as well not exist

§

reading, the mind
veers off the text, which becomes
marks on paper, re-entered
halfway through sense. what else
goes on in the interim:
fancy, lists of things undone,
thought of friends, music,
absorption of light, the sun
already its apex. a brief
moment of concentration, timed
to the washing cycle, the beat
of domesticity.

§

The fog fell again yesterday afternoon. You could see it descending towards the bus as we climbed Whitstable Rd towards the University. It's only lifting now, the following afternoon, though it's still dull.

when the students leave the rabbits return

cistern trickle

preternatural stillness
                      a man with a huge nose
walks his dog past the Farmhouse

§

brown bears (on the Continent) not hibernating
plants flowering out of season
(and an article on Brueghel: the *novelty* of snow in the Low Countries,
fake Alps in the background)

everyone's in the same boat (stranded airline passenger)

§

dark tunnels of trees on the Sandwich Road now let in light
(shopping in No Name Street on the shortest day)

§

I'm more aware than ever
of the fragility of lives, friendships
spread across the globe

fog grows denser here
                      (Rosemary driving to Whitstable
for a night meeting)

a light from a kitchen (that's me

at this moment), cooking (& what
anthropologists make of this)

One gets a sense of the smallness of this scene, this place, from Graham
Bennett's book on the Soft Machine: it's a story of the avant-garde
arriving in a village.

though why should 7/8 seem weird
amid irregular timber beams?

§

2 fat pigeons
1 blackbird (f, brown)
a squirrel

the ringing noise of what
seems like silence. is it produced
entirely in the ear? the tape hiss
of an unreliable recorder

a bird balances on the highest finger of a conifer

a car door slams

the few remaining students occasionally, and desultorily, out walking

the cloud almost mauve
the grass almost luminous

fingers flip
the book
no radio
no sign
or sound

§

waking up late:
the humans have stopped
                        (for Les Murray
'humans' became a term of abuse,
so what (who) was he
            a God?

—I just meant the rest of the world
went on as usual
                    though maybe lights
and the blow-up Santa Claus are a seasonal phenomenon
like nest-building—

                        a yellow American convertible
growls up the hill (a gift?) incongruous
amid salt bins and municipal bus shelters
                            (it should be populated
by Californians in striped shirts circa 1962
                            —be true to your school
like you would to your guy or girl—
                            or by some brilliantined loner
who will be pulled from the burning auto
up at the Eliot roundabout . . .
                    a good boy
to whom bad things had happened

                §

late morning
a continual complex pattern of bells,
sloe still on some hedges,
a mistle-thrush, mottled brown breast,
a broken down car en route to Bristol

a round
as I walk
around

(no sky for days)

drink Assam tea and
contemplate the future

on the path, a linnet, fawn with pink breast

§

Exit 9 to Twickenham, cross-country to Amersham, trying to remember the name of the nearby Quaker retreat (Jordans) just up the road from Milton's house (Chalfont St Giles).

Noted: for many English people of a certain class: the sense of service, the desire to work for charities and causes. It's probably a trait absent completely from those of working class background.

In Bushy Park (the Broom Clumps) Egyptian ducks, pheasants, a heron, luminous dogwood, acres of mud, ponds braced with sunken piles.

§

A bad dream in which I'm on a stage at a poetry reading in Australia, only to be told that I can't read my work because a lot of younger writers (who have completed degrees) need to read their work. The announcer hasn't heard of my work at all and what she sees of it is totally devoid of interest to her.

§

the wind sprang up
                and the wet
after a morning of sunlight

in the carpark, pied wagtails running
silvered tarmac
ravens
an albino squirrel

I'll stay in
and eat cold chicken

§

The modern part of Canterbury (south of the Cathedral, vicinity of St George's Place) was bombed out in 1940-43. Northgate and areas south and west bulldozed for the ring road in the 1960s. Station Rd West was extensively bombed, (and the site of a bus depot from 1935 until the 1990s.

Tyler Hill was Tile Kiln Hill c1819

no Great Houses in East Kent
where primogeniture was ignored

the year winds down

§

I could end with something portentous.

Or I could just do this:

January

New Year celebrations cancelled due to storms

the calendar:
                    Torres Strait carving
gives way to Iranian silk

an unaccustomed light in this room

§

A strange bird: me; 'strange' because here perhaps I am 'all show', not a characteristic I'd claim where I come from. But here, a bright squawking parrot.

best perhaps to take note of the interiors of churches

or take notes in their interiors
                        which we do
at Barfrestone (Norman circa 11-something)
a simple rectangular shell with decaying gargoyles.
Patrixbourne, up the road, we can't enter
though the shape seems unusual, the odd roof pitches,
a large square tower with timbered spire off-centre.
above the main door a man with florid moustache
amid mythical creatures. a thick layering of tiles
visible from the end of roofline—these overlap
more than I'd expect.
                        the villagers
in both cases probably *Telegraph* readers
(a silver sports car outside the Yew in Barfrestone)

on old maps, shifting nomenclatures and variant spellings
(the ghosting too of civic ambition:

streets gridded out in 1920 for a suburb
(of Whitstable) that never eventuated, the space
still rural on the current projection

how, over years
the names shift
a wood relocates
to the opposite side
of a village
a suburb suddenly
disappears then returns
in another place
even then, a title
confidently inked
proves a mistake
there was never
such a place, it
was hearsay

§

Driving across the North Downs, these unfenced single lanes with
infinite views. Hawthorn hedges—or fragments of them—then leaf
crops or ploughed fields, almost always a spire visible.

the angle of sun on brickwork
Roy Fisher's trajectory
                        clouds move rapidly
(storm warnings for the Channel)

A pheasant crosses the road, and it's all whitish down toward Canterbury,
darker and greener up at the roundabout.

§

a surface of moss,
miniature landscape of another planet,

its ridges and troughs in the slanting light
(in winter you always seem to be driving into the sun
when there is any)

I'm at the window in my Whistler's Mother position

A yellow band above the horizon against which the shapes of trees, bare
branches and pointed conifers, appear as the background of a renaissance
painting (or perhaps the fore-to-middle ground of a Paul Nash). But is it
the case that everything here is like something else? Is this why standard
English poetry is so fond of the simile?

Think of John Forbes' Switzerland: *a chocolate box at the speed of sound*

§

gulls circle at dawn

left completely alone we may not be happy but we do not disappear

§

June 1958: *The Hotel Wentley Poems*
received in today's post
from Lee Harwood. Who wouldn't want
to have written these? In 1958,
year of the Little Chef,
so why am I &c.
                        Buy underwear, socks,
Pan Am (the building) *is a colossal*
collection of minimums, so
Ada Louise Huxtable, *New York Times,* 1965
(relayed by Sebastian). But I am not American,
my poems contain no wild beestes, no
lady of the lake, I am
down the road (apiece) from the theatre
where crowds queued in 1963
for Cliff Richard's *Summer Holiday.*

§

everything back to normal
at the Goods Shed:
                  the two red headed and bearded butchers,
one, the son probably, a foot taller than the father,
intently dressing the cuts,
                  the fishmonger
reading the wrapping paper

§

            Gillingham is
            Jill, not Gill

            Teynham is
            Ten, not Tain

            Brize Norton is
            Eyes, not Ease

§

In the Museum Hotel, Bloomsbury, a loud Australian talks about
drinking, which is what you'd do in a John Forbes poem about London.
It's Friday night and the place crowds out. Too cramped to read a book.
It'd stick to the table anyway.

§

            They emerge from graves, Spencer's figures,
            as though lifted from bathtubs
            some hauled up by others
            (though are these holding coats?)
            some lift mounds of earth
            some drape themselves over headstones
            as though these have become divans
            some register surprise, others

seem to have just woken, fringed
by a natural world
                              a figure (the artist?),
right foreground, reclines
on a slab amid wildflowers

§

*What, I thought, is the future of this brightness? . . . Does it have to get 'out' of
the villages? . . . Wouldn't it be better to stay here, wouldn't it be better to get as
far away as possible, like Brisbane, or Capetown?*
                                                    —Peter Riley

the ungainly sprint of a young woman chasing a large plastic bag,
a large waddling man in a green jacket:
there is nothing 'out there' that is the 'material' for poetry

cherry trees blossom in the Big Apple

ewes lamb in December

§

take a short walk in the afternoon sun, staving off gloom

shapes of light and shade
translate to woodcut, a zigzag of dark on light green
orange—willow
off-white—birch
lime green—grass
china blue—sky
umber—everything else

                    now (4.15) pearl grey and
                    orange-pink
                    the street lights on

once these details were kept
for future use
                    a cycle
comprehended the odd inversion

§

Samuel Palmer's 'nature'
like an exploding *bottle of pop*

Remember that excellent remark of Mr B's—how that a tint equivalent to a
shadow is made by the outlines of many little forms in one mass, and then how
the light shines on the unbroken mass near it, such for instance as flesh . . .
                                                        —Palmer (1824)

a magpie flies into the wind with difficulty
clinging, leeward of a cypress,
days perceptibly lengthening

§

myth is a way of explaining, not a strategy,
as the figure is discovered in the ground?

a twitter in the bush beneath the *blasted oak*

St Hilary's Day, supposed to be the coldest in the year

parts of Hamburg under water

§

                    Broadstairs: Thanet's promenades
                    high above the beaches
                    every second object named
                    for Charles Dickens, the streets
                    as ramps for bored adolescents.

artificial light takes over early
here and at Ramsgate
where everything seems closed

a mirror in which Dickens may have seen himself,
a chair *like the empty chair*
in the painting by Luke Fildes
done after the subject's death

§

Le Tombeau de Ste Augustin.
layers of Augustine's temple:
three churches melding as one, then destroyed
(iconoclasm and earthquake
—one in the 17th century around Canterbury, apparently—

                               still, an arch, a wall,
the base of an octagonal structure (that may never have been completed)

§

'trivia'—a meeting of three streets

assemble and
dissemble

the bus stop, an
extra-terrestrial light box

the sphere, the cylinder, the cone,
the café at 9 am.

Futurist Poets!
the vapour trails you only imagined
are indeed beautiful, and yes
the sky is our canvas
(though it may kill us)

§

Faversham: 'The Sun'
opposite 'West House' (now
'Cancer Research UK')
                          porter
and old maps (Thames Estuary)

today our 'fate' is sealed, the piece of paper
that will allow an exchange of documents

this, I must remind myself
is 'my street', and this
'my local'

this, in the English tradition
is my second living room

§

I keep thinking notebooks like this were kept once by the lunatics
who'd frequent the City of Sydney Public Library. They would write IN
CAPITALS (like Billy Jones, though a lot less interesting).

§

over the hill to the North Sea
(cloud lifts, then there's a strand of cobalt,
then paler blue, then the sea itself, a nondescript brown-green

further, white shapes of wind turbines

in Whitstable's main street the screech
of swinging pub signs
(not 'swinging pubs')

birds fly backwards

an old woman, encased
in a clear plastic umbrella

could roofs lift?   or cars?   mine?

that greyhound, almost a flying pooch . . .

out over the sea, great clouds of spray

a grandfather holds a child
like a child holds a balloon

and yet a gull moves forward,
able to use the wind

from here the turbines are mere suggestions
charcoal lines almost

(birds flying with the wind, are they exhilarated?)

§

a fox, caught
in headlights
walks away
across the car park

after a large dinner (out), I'm bilious, confined (mostly) to bed, after
sending several dyspeptic emails

steamed rice
a banana

Samuel Palmer
by Timothy Wilcox

in 1788, gleaning
rendered illegal

and in 1832
rick burning, des-
truction of farm equipment

the bucolic became unfashionable

Palmer got to Rome
just as a taste for the oriental took hold

§

finally, the cold weather
a thin bird out there
(a touch of red
or it's just the light)
flies up, then drops
from a pine branch

fly right
write well
(say the Andrews Sisters)

§

do I repeat myself?
very well then, I repeat myself.
I am small,
I have blackouts

please call 999 in case of emergency
or keep reading this poem
remembering these lines
as if they were your own

§

Each week a new moral panic. The Home Office followed by Big Brother. Today's non-news: *the 22nd of January is the most depressing day of the year* (followed by a feature on 'getaways').

§

> wind through gaps in the wall
> (plug these with paper towel)
>
> a new cloud formation,
> pale glow under a grey band
> fuzzed at the edges

§

Congratulations! You have won a kilo of sweet potatoes!

§

Rosemary returns from a lecture
delivered by someone *untroubled by literature*

this seems for a moment an idyllic state

§

A Philosopher wd laugh at my reckoning a house an important Object, but I am not a Philosopher, & whoever is not, is apt to consider things according to their bulk, & I am sure in that view my House is not a bagatelle
—Elizabeth Montagu

What would Ken make of the Goods Shed, a Baci of One's Own (?), ceiling heaters some ten feet above. From metal poles on chains: bouquets of hops (?), chillies, ham legs, a mosquito net, a fish trap, a lost umbrella. A new lunch menu about to materialise—chalk on a drying slate comes to life as the 10.50 for Charing Cross pulls in. salt scattered on the platform looks like snow, but it isn't yet.

A kingfisher arcs along the Stour near the middle of town, under the bridges and over the locks

on the road back from Sandwich
flurries (windscreen iced up
overnight)
        the strangeness of driving
through white dots

§

Still working on the poem ('One-Way Ticket'). The parts alright (mostly), but not the whole.

it doesn't cohere (?)

rather, it's a labyrinth, confusing but leading somewhere

(the grey sky suddenly becomes very white, though the cloud is no less thick)

maybe we are fading out?

awaiting the next movie?

with the whiteness, silence in the auditorium

then the milk truck arrives

§

It's quiet in the Miller's Arms, Monday afternoon after the washing. Quiet too out on St Radigund's, the street that might have been a ring-road.

the spine cracks as I straighten up

                             (there's a red house

over yonder

                         and a red-cheeked woman pushing a pram laden
with paper—I mean artificially red-cheeked, almost clown-like, lipstick
approximating to lips, dyed orange hair.

down the road, scaffolds, as a roof is replaced—this (literal) backwater
of the Stour

§

Alan Sillitoe's guide to the Saxon Shore Way—he passed through
Faversham; stayed at the (now defunct) Ship Inn on Market Square. His
style, strangely stilted and impersonal for a 'working class writer'.

§

fear of purchasing white goods
fear of a sofa not fitting

post fifty letters
dismantle several typewriters

§

         measuring   measuring

the way a space always looks smaller when empty

John, the antique dealer next door: *this place is on the way up* with the
unvoiced *know wot I mean?*

and us a part of this gentrification—I am a Doctor

                  'welcome'
as a friend said
            'to village life'

February

Green moss on tree trunks glows in sunlight
(the Greenwood?)

What will fit in the house?
What is that smell—something dead—under the kitchen floor?
                                                                It's
strange to unpack crockery, the sheer volume of things once lived with.

Suddenly we have several sets of keys.

§

Late train (and bus—track work) back from London. On the train, a
guy in black plastic trousers and overcoat (designer label: NECESSARY
EVIL, which Rosemary parses as NECESSARY VINYL). Long black hair
and a (very English) bald spot. I wear my hood up in the cold, thinking
someone might see me as a characteristic 'hoodie' then I'd turn around
and I'd be a horrible old guy like Death in the Bergman movie.

would Alan Gould write a poem about this?

§

English sunlight on Afghan carpet
(this is postcolonialism)

the backyard snow-covered,
footprints and bike tracks down West St,
blurred white outside the window

Albert Einstein passes by

what are those hooks on the front of the public bar?

§§§

Interlude: Marrakech

my glasses taken away to be
mysteriously mended (orientalism?)
I can't see what I write
(so how do I know what I say . . .?)

a strange bird above the canopy of the *riad*.
what's it like out there
in the lanes we traversed last night
and how will we find our way back here?

                               with difficulty,

from the square, 'Assembly of the Dead',
adjacent to the *Jardin Foucault*

§

             as those rugs
             this journal
             woven or knotted

enmeshed in the processes of capital,
services (like products) invented;
in the *souk*: more things you don't want
than you could imagine
                     motorcycles
like a fantasy of friends turning up
on two wheels in a French movie sometime in the 1960s
magnified a thousand-fold

the museum must be somewhere
but—don't ask

§

in the pink city, beaks clack
(stork nests on the walls of the old palace).

Evening up on the roof with the satellite dishes, the Atlas Mountains beyond. Car horns and *muezzin* feedback (amplified voices for 360 degrees), a light at the top of the Bab Doukkala mosque.

Islam forbade the illustration of humans and animals but not plants— but then plants are the closest living things to writing, and the two often grow inseparable.

cirrus inscriptions across the sky

§

up in the bedroom, while the others,
drunk on fig alcohol, resound from the courtyard

> *malade*
> I attempt coffee
the limbs ache, and the stomach
can contain no more

Marrakech in the cool of the morning

a small bird flies in and out
of the room

> my soul, probably

intricate ceilings

> or, Johnny Kidd & the Pirates:
achin all over

> lattice

(*let us pray*)

or, *mashrabbiya*

blue vase-work and
gold orbs

today, the inner world
(not venturing into the *medina*)

§

everyone else has gone to the waterfalls

The sun too intense to share with rooftop cats for more than a few
minutes, descend to Michel's music in the courtyard: Django Reinhardt,
Bessie Smith, Debussy, sounds of Morocco.

cool wind from the mountains,
a distant traffic snarl

3 pm, I warm myself on the roof again
balancing sunglasses above reading glasses,
a large insect on a leather recliner

scent of cooked meats and sewage

§

each morning a slower start

In an olive grove, midday, no shade
and a heat in late winter that makes you wonder what summer must be
like. Later, the *Jardin Majorelle*, former hiding place of Yves St Laurent, a
house behind a gas station where St Laurent downed his two bottles of
scotch a day.

pique-niques et chiens interdits

in between,
the boredom of the new town,
later,
the insanity of the old.

Went home, said Evelyn Waugh (in Abyssinia),
sacked my servants

on the roof,
we watch the swallows,
watch the stars
(Venus and Orion)

fly me to the moon

§

what is a bargain?
the vertebra of a whale?
the spine of a salesman?

fifty percent off a life of reduced options?

meanwhile, high-school French
(all I remember
of an early textbook:
*Voici d'abord
la tête de Claude*

of use in surreal emergencies

Today it was hot, or supposed to be, in the *souks*, but a breeze lifted it and
we sat on the roof of *Chez Chagrouni* in amber light, haze surrounding
the city we will return from, with
a little joie de vivre
(*not* contraband)
which will, at a pinch,
fit a suitcase

§

as in the square
in the *riad*:
fire-dancing and shoes
against paving
the tunings, footfall
and hand-jive of a wider informing culture,
Africa, America, and now us:
freed from Occupational Health and Safety
we celebrate Helen's fifty years

a swirl, a dance
to which I am not a contributor
unless in this
                          the lights
float on the pool
                          things may come and things may go
but the art school dance goes on forever
as though, in the crowd
you recognise Sigmund Freud, Vladimir Lenin,
George Formby.
                          writing is a thing apart,
that thing through which these things
now sing
                that once were bodies moving

Free your mind and your ass will follow

my 'ass' perhaps
                (maybe not my stomach)

wagged (like Jarvis Cocker's at a Michael Jackson concert)

                                    (the belly dancer's invitation)

[end interlude]

§§§

floor appears, on which to place carpet

the gradual diminution of boxes (still
unpacking my library)

It's a long way from Marrakech (though the appeal of that town predicates
on its bohemian history and that comes down to the availability of boys
and *kif*. Strange that the respectable middle-class should get off on this
while dodging the rotting vegetables and *souk* hustlers.

In, On or About the Premises

in an old photograph,
the pub's ingle-nook

                    two gents, behatted
                    in the fireplace

it's W H Auden's 100th birthday
(and Robert Mugabe's 83rd)

my prescription, courtesy *the good Sir Jesse Boot*,
cement delivered, garbage disposed, plumbing . . .

                              The Romantics didn't have
to worry about any of this, but look what happened to Lord Byron . . .

put another log on the fire

                    toosh

(Lord Byron, Live at the Club Foote?)

There are stretches of the town where you can step back into the 1930s
or 1950s then out again . . . to the 18th century.

The narrowness of West Street, a way, now pedestrianised, to the middle
of town. Lights in the opposite windows like a stage set. Everything here
is like a stage set:

this is why LANGUAGE poetry exists

snow?
         we've probably seen the last (and first) of it, but
the stage set:
I like it
         the way everything in life, as Jonathan Williams observed,
begins to resemble *Coronation Street*.

a woman walks in carrying a heavy mirror

the pub is full of teachers

                what most students want to do on a field trip
is get absolutely shit-faced

§

an unidentified flower emerges in the backyard
(after the daffodils two weeks back).
in the park, the first hawthorn blossom

poems from various people: Pam, Angela, Jaya (now in Rome)

§

a walk around the town's perimeter,
move several boxes,
lay cement,
hang pictures,
listen to *50,000 Fall Fans Can't Be Wrong*

§

Last night, the movies. The local picture theatre seems to have been in operation since the thirties at least: art deco with heraldry. The audience for the film (*Notes on a Scandal*) represent the bourgeoisie of Faversham—the 'art-loving' end of it (though the woman behind us 'tsk tsks' at Cate Blanchett on the toilet, then snores through the end of the movie). Stepping out into the street afterwards was like entering a film set. You expected 1940s people to materialise in big curvy cars, everyone with hats.

but it was 2007

it *is* 2007

three men in plastic macs arrive

(*how I wrote 'elastic man'*)

§

       spice shop =
       (hos)pice shop

            an English version
of Blackburn's *zen food* (fro-)

       it's washing day

this Friday I read in London

On the day of the tube bombings everyone just went to the pub.

§

    gusts of rain,
    white blossoms,

broken vacuum cleaner
missing squeeze-mop (!)

hello Philip Whalen!

March

settling in

a bright, perfectly clear day

Basil's *77 Beasts*:
his work, by accumulation,
detail magnified, or shifted

a painting, viewed
in different surrounds

the shadow of a lamp, its reflected light
cast upward on the shop wall

                the way such a dark presence in
Chiroco's painting might emanate from another time, be a trace rather
than the immediate effect of an unseen object

THE THING! (writ in dripped blood)

§

By Hollowshore and the Ham Marshes, against a stiff wind along the
muddy top of a dyke. Down Oare Creek and up Faversham Creek, the
skeletal spire never out of sight. Off the dyke, at low tide, crescent bogs,
startled waders, the stiles ('lovers' gates') always a mud patch. Closer to
Faversham, the shipyards, then diversion around new housing to Front
Brents.

§

Tiepolo and the defeat of gravity:
that we should see the great event from beneath,

earthbound, while they float upward;
this, at Dulwich Gallery, an afternoon
waiting for Canaletto (a lesser artist
though one whose work reveals more about
the desires of an age

                              property and spectacle
no longer containable by ordinary perspective
the fish-eye takes even more in,
those flecks, humans, on artificial
Venetian waters that lap to formula
under equally invariable skies

§

Gloria Petyarre's print
now radiant over the bedend

Walala Tjapaljarri's very 'male' painting,
wants to elbow the others aside, have
a wall to itself

§

the ends of fingers crack, lose sense of touch

the madness of March
                              (hatters and hares)
and the point, seven months in, of this notebook,
that the seasons don't work.

but that, precisely, is where I began

March: the month of prose

§

It's apparent that the past (for all its charm) is something you suffer
(heritage listings, quirky disfunction). This is on par with grain-fed

venison and fair-trade coffee. The middle-classes must suffer for their gain (the upper classes just open it all up to the public).

previously unnoticed, behind the bar of the Miller's Arms
a photograph of the Sydney Opera House

§

East Kent, is (mostly) NT-free
from where
the M-25 goes everywhere

(a Home County Haiku)

every evening around six
the door to the video shop
slams frequently

(almost a song)

diminished expectations?
a mess of pottage?
a pot of basil?

(things to do in Faversham)

from David Miller, his new Selected Poems, *In the Shop of Nothing*
(some people will shop at nothing)

laughter at the bar

(those guys in the hearth
must have been small

the surprising thinness of French wine

écriture

> I am a book,
> a *livre*,
> a lever
>
> aleatory
>
> a liver?

§

The British Library: a display of Gael Turnbull's Migrant Press with related items, collaborations, Gael's later work, the Mallarmé dice, the folded *As From a Fleece*.

Renoir at the National Gallery (and Leon Kossoff's studies of works in the collection: *an artist's impression* says Ken). Renoir at a loss with vast spaces (sky, sea), more at home where minute variations and details are possible though nonetheless he smudges these. It's all spring and summer and some of it is sketchier than reproduction suggests, fawn canvas showing through often. You become aware of the audacity of these practices in 1870. It's hard to imagine what could be so disruptive now (or since, say, 1930). We manufacture our own notoriety; they lived through theirs.

Hogarth at the Tate Britain: 'character' v 'caricature'
the best paintings are the portraits.

§

Early Bird and the window open
(spring brew and climate control)
the grate scraped out, though a cold snap's
on the way. A small table squared up

makes me feel like an 18th century
automaton, the 'writer-at-a-desk' figure, bewigged
(bothered and bewildered?) as I write to
my dispersed auditors.

John Seed stresses the importance
of words on paper, contra the emphasis on sound and performance
(since Bunting). The Migrant Press display gave this argument strength
or presented examples: the artist collaborations, the mere presence of
specks on paper, on screen.

the image of Gael as an enlightenment figure:
a photomontage with the caption
change the world / hard enough to write this

§

the last bottle of HP sauce comes off the line in Birmingham

§

dust in the garage, ivy
creeping under the weatherboards

Europe will be a desert in forty years

The youth of Faversham pass down this street on Friday nights in search
of what? What can 'heritage' offer them?

better rap
than rep

I like the vicarious sense of jollity these places engender. I could call this
a solitary practice but it isn't. It reverberates in odd rooms around the
globe.

the continuity: what I write in a pub in Kent is read in an office in Adelaide,
a pensione in Rome, an internet café in the Blue Mountains, an apartment
in upstate New York.

then the paper boy borrows my pencil

(that trio: Blackburn, Creeley, Sorrentino now gone)

to keep track of what?

a sign reads: *Respect Our Neighbours / Please Leave Quietly*
(but I *am* the neighbours)

(I am, perhaps, *Neighbours*)

§

People who don't write think of writing as some wonderful emanation, something the author has to get down. Images in film of the writer urgently scribbling. But what if the writing is like *this*, a writing that *pushes* itself along? What if the writer has to force him/her self to write? This is writing as 'work', something the writer may not actually want to be doing. It becomes enjoyable at the editorial stage when all these dull slugs of prose seem to 'light up', escaping their humdrum origins. This is the point at which the writing becomes something *other* than the travail of the writer. It is also the point at which writing is abandoned (though with pleasure often) by the one who might otherwise make a claim for it. It then appears (perhaps) perversely under the author's name but the name at this point has become a mere signifier (if you liked _____'s _____, you'll like their _____). Marshall Berman wrote about the artist character's desire to *see his name in lights*, the modern signifier of success. Mostly we see ours on flickering screens.

§

on the high banks of railway cuttings
the beginnings of leaves

though High Street Chatham's
a chill gorge

uphill to the war memorial
a fat bumblebee inert on the path

§

If I can't email somebody I realise suddenly I can *phone* them!

I sense what Tom Raworth must have felt about the apparatus of poetry and the poetry world. Why, once installed in a prestigious position he chose to write things that defied what an ensconced poet might be expected to produce. I am not such a perfectionist.

§

What does one person's knowledge amount to?

§

Early flowers—daffodils (or 'Lent lilies') and primulas (primroses = *prima rosa*)—in this case 'rhubarb and custard', joined by a small purple flower, something yellow on a bush and a creeper that looks suspiciously like blooming. New leaves on a rose bush. A hanging rose. Further bulbs—iris? (or poppies). Some clover (?). Low-lying plants (perhaps herbs), acanthus, other less visible varieties.

Cut back the ivy at ground level but be careful further up in case of nests (this can wait till autumn), taking the weight off the trellis.

§

a pub hubbub

hanging dogs
on short leashes

a woman presses her breasts against the window
(for her companion to kiss?)

§

John Seed spoke against punctuation. He's right for his own practice, the idea that one should set things so that they read *so*. But I have to put this in italics. When I began to write I decided at one point to stop using punctuation until I found there was a real reason to use it. Then I reached a point, years later, when I wanted a kind of Enlightenment absence of ambiguity for which punctuation was crucial. Partly this came from reading Robert Browning's 'Sordello' (as recommended by Ezra Pound). Contemporary critics had lambasted Browning for his incomprehensibility but if you observed the punctuation everything, however convoluted, made perfect sense.

On the sound system, Labelle: *voulez vous couchez avec moi, ce soir* (the comma or pause is important, as Andrew Ford noted when scanning my song '(Do the) Modernism' (*and the name of the dance is the* (pause) *Modernism*). He knew this gap was there despite the absence of punctuation.

§

at Rochester, battlements in chill wind
and the winding High Street
a choir beginning in the cathedral
whose walls testify to the marriage
of religion and imperialism
(successive wars in Afghanistan,
1830s and 1870s,
and still they're there.

Rochester never went anywhere near the place (Rochester)

The outskirts of industrial towns like Sittingbourne: what Henri Lefebvre meant by 'housing'—the place you put people in their 'non-productive' hours.

§

hit on the head
by a falling bed
the perils of D.I.Y. (A falling bedhead in fact. The skull escaping fracture.
The furniture ending up in the right place)

stinging nettles in the garden, discovered by accident.

§

A thing learnt with age: to appear interested. But we all know that's
what the other person is doing. This is 'manners'.

I remember talking thugs—university boys—out of throwing Landon
Watts out of a gig in the Sydney Union—it was XTC with an unlikely
and inappropriate support act—must have been 1978?

It was eloquence I would normally have lacked.

But where am I now? In a town the size of Bairnsdale with four times as
many pubs. Canterbury would be the size of Bathurst.

It's the old who drink alone, like that gent in a suit up at the bar.

I think of John Forbes' small *oeuvre* compared to my own sprawl. Was it
that he knew what poetry was and I don't? He felt it was his own task to
edit the work (as a whole). I'm not so certain.

§

Whittard's, Canterbury

rooftops and skylights beneath unmitigated grey

Japanese green tea restores the spirits

and suddenly it's evening

April

Immigrant Spring Poem:

When the [   ] sings before dawn
from the branches of the [   ]
the blue [   ]s unfurl
while grey [   ]s circle in the skies

§

At the rear of West Street an old estate wall. The buildings impinge upon each other, a stairwell into the neighbour room, a cellar under a different space. What's now the garage used to be a bakery (the house was a fishmonger's).

§

From the Ham Marshes you can navigate by the church spire: Faversham's open frame, visible from Hollowshore, the Shipwright pub.

clap hands to make the young bulls move on
(other side of the lovers' gate)

§

In the stationers I view maps on the first floor, viewed myself by the security camera. The shop's proprietor comes upstairs and pretends to do odd tasks but is really just making extra sure I don't steal anything.

Sometimes it seems this whole small world belongs to the National Trust and you will be able to buy preserves and tea-towels at the kiosk afterwards.

§

send photographs to various people,
of this house, its particularity,
the warp in the floor, the curvature of walls

the poets are mostly silent, things close down at Lent

§

*Painting which looks as if it's made through gritted teeth isn't the only kind
that's worth attention.* (1943)

*To give yourself completely to what you're doing while simultaneously watching
yourself do it—that's the hardest of all for those who work by instinct.* (1912)
—Matisse

§

back lanes to the Chart Gunpowder Mill
following the creek through Davington
then uphill to the cricket ground
overlooking the Almshouses.
Davington Pond, the allotments,
the back of a supermarket

clear nettles and dead leaves from the path
(these leftovers from last year)

take the doors off their hinges

(useless doors to the living room
detach of their own accord when opened)

§

Distanced from Kenneth Slessor and Christopher Brennan, the latter
more of an acquired taste (not mine). You have to admire Slessor for
the way he worked in isolation. None of his friends had the faintest
idea of what he really thought; the poems got by them through force

of their author's personality (none of them would have countenanced Eliot). I keep thinking of Slessor playing Douglas Stewart a Kurt Weill record. Stewart thought it was a practical joke. But why does Slessor erupt here?

§

Of all noxious animals too the most noxious is a tourist. And of all tourists the most vulgar, illbred, offensive and loathsome is the British tourist.

—Francis Kilvert (1870)

§

at Knole, the weight of history,
the rotting canopy of a four-poster

those fearsome kings and clerics
—enough to bury Vita Sackville-West
were she given the chance
                              (how could Knole
be regretted?

                    adjourn
for lunch, Shoreham,
a fold in the North Downs,
the Darent
           —no trace
of Samuel Palmer, *the most excellent*
Mr B.
           a footpath, signed
under ten feet of water

further up the road,
                    Lullingstone,
its mosaics and hot baths out of place
in this landscape

                                   then, nowhere,
                    the approach to Dartford,
                    chapels lost with infill

                    it's Easter

                    day of the exploding coffee-pot

                                   §

At Winchelsea, the site of a windmill destroyed in the storms of 1987, as
the fallen trees of Knole, only a grindstone and some foundation slabs
next to a trig point up above the marshes.

                    Ford Madox Ford's house,
                    in a back street (the town
                    strangely without shops; a pub
                    that pretends to have lunch reservations)

                    Rye, choked with traffic,
                    a haze across the marsh

                    Bank Holiday: a motorcyclists' convention

                    from Rye Harbour, Camber Sands
                    dotted with bathers, the nuclear plant
                    at Dungeness

                                   §

                          write, he said,
                          poetry, that sense
                          follow sound, not
                          endless digression
                          the quagmire of
                          expository prose
                          instead this

this this (as if
you knew it, what
it was. instead it's
a chain of un-
being, dis-
connection, a place
for which there's no
vocabulary, a set
of images, not
the one sharp thing, the
light in this room
nebulous, the space
between other things.

§

bluebells, tulips, climbing plants (honeysuckle), a holly bush that needs

pulling out

cinerarias, potted, in the window

a car alarm in the Faversham night

what dumb music?!

and the days go by . . . and the days go by
(why I am not a painter)

pull out the holly, roots deep
under stone

wash clothes

how much of this
already structured,
an idea, not a thing
(though ideas are things)?

§

a finger, trimmed
with secateurs
makes for shaky writing

spring, season of accidents

(incident / accident, it's
all the same in Italian)

(the geranium incident)

1698
a salve
a salvo
salute!

the Bird, or
the Bishop's Finger

either way
I'm all thumbs

settling after, to read
the origins of disco,
subversions of dance

things that happened
while I gazed at my shoes

§

The world of these first years in Nice is a world behind glass . . . the world infinitely repeated in a kind of insistent, existential loss. As if the light one had to obtain resulted in nothing but solitude, and demanded a fatal renunciation.
—Dominique Fourcade on Matisse

§

cuttings, dead leaves
from two seasons back
bagged
      tulips
now open, yellow,
streaked with red

a fragment of glass
under the end ridge tile

take the sun, before
it disappears behind
a neighbour chimney

signs of life: clematis
honeysuckle

the chimney shade angles
across the terrace, light
full on the wall
with the hanging rose

heavy scent of malt
from Shepherd Neame

a fine evening
and a very quiet night ahead

§

. . . the house was still
and quiet
      (a children's book read in the bar)

Sitting in the yard this afternoon I'm beginning to be convinced that I'm
actually here for the foreseeable future.

                    (the garden still
and quiet, save the drone of a bumble-bee)

help! I'm becoming a Georgian!
(nature and the pub tempered by cyberspace)

gillyflowers high on the walls

this is where I live
this is who I am

§

        a television 'black hole'
        (our place in its midst)

        Madness! I mean Madness, not
        madness (playing in the bar)

        North Sea wind takes the warmth
        out of the warmth

        opposite Front Brents, photographing mud

        am I losing weight?

        are friends electric?

        could I make a book
        called 'Sequiturs'?

§

The response to Matisse's work: that it looked terrible, but then
everything around it started to look dull. Then, almost at the moment of
acceptance his work was seen as retrograde, the Cubists and Surrealists
had seen to that (though Breton had earlier championed him). The

paintings done in Nice in the 1920s, products of existential terror viewed as comfortable domesticity.

horror vacui

Hilary Spurling attributes Matisse's twenties 'orientalism' as much to the developing cinema industry in the South as to earlier visits to North Africa. The drapes and 'sets' within the apartment owed as much to the sets observed out in the streets.

§

a suicide bomber in Bagdhad's parliament

mysterious death of bee colonies

the 'terror' is a constant (the 1970s a lapse, otherwise
it's been this way since 1914)

§

out on the stones (the tiles?),
a sheltered place in the yard
(no thinning here of the bee population)

the profusion of plants, their shapes,
reminds of Albrecht Dürer,
that obsessive detail (Dürer
or a spliffed up Billy Jones)

smoke from an unknown source
(farmers burning off, still?)

§

An afternoon spent on an Islington balcony to the distant sounds of Arsenal, the tube crowded later with red shirts. Today, in the heat, to

Chilham, a walk through Godmersham Park and back through Ridge Wood, carpeted with bluebells. Mail from Ken. An article from the *Adelaide Monthly* on the appearance of a certain French painter—Mr Goggin—from the South Seas, visiting Masonic contacts early in 1903.

§

                    bird tracks on
                    mudbanks
            a river
            repeating itself
                    Wordsworth *nosing through*
                    the shallows of art (the revised
                    'Prelude')
                            the year
                            the calendar
            a flimsy excuse

                    lying in this bed, naked at 10 pm,
                    the room still hot

                            to step into
                            Gloria Petyarre's
                            landscape, or
                            the other side of the glass
                            painted on by Loma Bridge

                                    where has the bravado
                                    of the 1970s gone?

§

Found, as a placemark in Louis MacNeice's *Collected Poems*, a receipt from Tranby Aboriginal Cooperative.

The train approaches London. Quickly. Slowly.

§

A duck on the garage roof, and one below in the yard (yesterday morning a group of mallards asleep in the middle of Thomas Rd).

The last light
in the upstairs bedroom

smeared windows

equilibrium

§

in the Anchor, end of Abbey St
reading maps of Brighton / Hove
and Gravesend / Rochester
positioning roads and villages
observed from the train,
the way their relationship alters
between view and diagram

black ink appears grey
on yellow paper
(smudge)
the darkness is absorbed
leaving a penumbra on the page

a long gallery between bars
appears as a mirror image
but the space is actual (the chairs
are different, a lampshade
not reflected elsewhere.
one clear window amid the frosted
views the street towards the town centre,
past the house of Arden
(*Arden of Faversham*)

§

Stonehenge from a distance appears like a replica of itself; around the standing stones the lesser verticals of tour groups.

haze, descending into Somerset

          at Beer Head, the cliffs, red and white
          the distant wreck of the *Napoli*
          cranes in position, listing to starboard off Branscombe beach

          Ottery St Mary, the green man
          and the elephant man, both
          beneath the painted cross-beams of the church
          (clover, stars and *fleurs-de-lis*),
          the clock a calendar, various members
          of the Coleridge family

crushed leaves of dock alleviate the sting of nettles

          obsessive ceilings (the Victorians
          particularly the Arts and Crafts types
          at Knightshayes, these
          boarded over only years after completion,
          discovered a century later

          the Victorians cushioned by stuff
          the *bric-a-brac* of empire, this
          maybe the true origin
          of modernism *and* 'postmodernism':
          things forced into genre

After which we are lost on the roundabouts and one-ways of Tiverton, forced to travel south when we want east.

§

Things grow measurably the three days we're away.

It's the anniversary of the Kinder mass-trespass. Various accounts appear in the papers. Yorkshire singer Mike Harding organises a concert. But one reviewer notes that the legacy of open country is its current takeover by the middle-class. Indeed this is true (expensive real-estate, the tone of NT and Heritage literature). The working classes who may have had a shack near the beach found themselves threatened with demolition orders for desecrating the landscape. And it's now expensive to leave town (outrageous rail fares &c). The trespass can only carry its legacy where it remains possible to walk out of a city.

§

it's a difficult transition
into this mannered landscape,
but do I mind my own nuances?

not really

John Forbes! where are you now!
and how would you situate yourself
amidst this: the consequence
of Empire
                    (that some of 'us'
come 'back',
Windrush and Earl's Court
and so it goes
                    (we become
annoying columnists and book reviewers,
or rather our predecessors do, or did
(*not me, not my good intentions*)

§

Walk through the dull backblocks of Faversham parallel to the Whitstable Road. Cross the railway and through fields, rape, hops and corn, to the church at Goodnestone. The path loses itself on a modern farm. Ford a small stream, then up a hill alongside cherry trees and across the motorway to Fostal and Hernhill, its village square. Through the Mount Ephraim Gardens to Boughton and a bad pub (The Queens's Head).

No matter how accurate the map there's always a point where you get lost.

§

recipes, lists, dream journals

§

Upstairs at 8.15 am, the Kent earthquake. 4.5 on the Richter scale, epicentre: Folkestone. Then a walk from Selling station up through orchards to Perry Wood. Along a ridge, views out to Lees Court (W) and (S) over Shottenden, the rape fields.

birch, holly, rowan

Down a steep slope then up another to view an earthwork, then down into Selling itself, through Gushmere, and across the railway to Boughton Church. Then through a golf course to the village.

§

how diffuse the light, a bright blue day
with cold northerly gusts

move to the south side of the house
from which to watch, but not feel the briskness

the sway of a fruit tree two doors up

a small dog, nails
slipping on floorboards

the light hangs around
as I check maps, locations for tomorrow's walk

the minimum of drear infill

§

Our house was once one half of next door which is now half of the door after, if that makes sense. The original wide doors no longer open, due to subsidence. This is the origin of 'flying freehold' (their cupboard opens onto the wall of our stairs; the internal entry to the cellar is theirs, the external ours—a new internal built subsequently). The old beams mostly salvaged from ships, hence the curved shapes and the slots for cross timbers. The ships predating the building a century or more (deforestation already a problem?).

§

a puma, rumoured once
in Canterbury

May

in the middle of Blean Woods
on the Red Road (a track)
photograph nailed to a trunk, flowers,
Simon, another year,
in all our hearts, done
as though a roadside death but
in the middle of a wood.
how did this happen?

Arrive at the Red Lion, Hernhill, *too soon, too late* though they pour me a pint before they close. I sit on a bench with umbrella shade facing the green and the church with its surprisingly dull interior.

From Fostal the rights of way are overgrown skirting Horse Hill, gunshots as a farmer scares birds off the crop. After Graveney it's easier going. Pigeons explode from hedges. Then the dyke path up Faversham Creek.

large cyclists in floral shorts,
(the dream of wearing sandals and socks forever?)

William Cobbett would have been appalled by the countryside now, bright with rape fields and acres of plastic sheeting.

§

Coast walk, Margate to Broadstairs. Margate will *not* be the new Brighton: it faces north. Bungalows thin out towards North Foreland, then, past Botany Bay, the landscape is invaded by gullies. Thereon the residences are larger, walled off (the sea also).

At Broadstairs lunch next door to Neptune's Hall, across the road from Barnaby Rudge. The burger without cheese is without anything else though it is 'locally sourced'. In the bookshop, volumes piled high on the floors; a bookseller who makes grunting noises.

On the train back: a Scottish alcoholic and junkie, in and out of rehab, off to Gillingham to appear in a line-up. He'd punched someone in a pub and could remember nothing of it. Talked about being on probation and trying unsuccessfully to kick both habits. Middle-class parents who live in Florida, plus a couple of brothers and sisters. He gets the conductor to plug in his mobile for a recharge after people on the station (Margate) weren't helpful. 'This is Tony Blair' he said. I said 'what, your mobile doesn't work and it's Tony Blair?' He shook my hand effusively before I got off the train.

§

driven half crazy
by plumbing
                    I learn
how to drain a radiator,
how not to fill a boiler

where's the poetry in that?

§

Making coffee, the interruptions, small fragments that compose a life.

Q: What are you going to do with it (your life)?

A: At 1.08 catch the train to London to look at the Russian Futurists.

Remember the way one sentence would follow another?

blueness, redness, yellowness

you write
against the grain, against
the draining board

                    bluebells,
an odd buttercup

thistles

the dyslexic street

                (Canonbury, not

Canterbury)

                (as the proof-reader substitutes

yolk for yoke)

the Bureau has ordered the rains to come,
sparrows scratch in the dirt,
rattle the gutters.

§

Goncharova's paper-cuts for *Victory over the Sun*, the costumes,
the way futurism (and the Russians)
looked back as much as forward
(peasant clothes, for their 'modernity',
the horse rather than the motor car)

though don't we all do this:
envisage a future with components of the past?
and then that 'future' begins to resemble the present of its conception

§

the street dead quiet (Bank Holiday),
across the road a bad painting
looks like someone in a red apron
clutching a skeletal iguana
(further clues concealed by a curtain)

§

The Bishop of S_____, accosted months back trying to break into a car
while incapacitated said *I'm the Bishop of S_____. It's what I do.* The case
was quietly dropped.

§

The 'future' of the Futurists was largely the absence of a past. They recreated the winged victory as a fast car, as if, like the symbolists, speed itself, an idea, meant more than the thing. So—lines of force. Synaesthesia: coloured music, the curve (of beauty?) as well as the diagonal and the triangle.

Then Marinetti, at sixty, enlisting, or trying to; Boccioni killed by accident, not warfare.

The dimmers come on. But we are Futurists in here! We demand light: the assassination of the moon! Death by vapour trail!

I'm not exactly observing my surrounds, but this *is* a theatre, a space, open, for whatever takes are taken.

Harry's avant-garde sensibilities: that one must be open always to performance (this may be Futurism's real legacy, those eruptions of sound, those uncontrollable musics.

The notebook too needs its infusions, its discrete noises. Discredited modernity doesn't mean a retreat to *chaise longue* and chesterfield.

§

a wet afternoon in London,
a phalanx of taxis
out in New Oxford Street

people pass this window with secret smiles

tonight, Christopher Middleton reads
or if he doesn't, I do (like Aerosmith
subbing for the Rolling Stones?)

§

I'm pissed off with myself for several reasons . . .
I left it, packed, on the platform

Mine ended up on the other side of Kent

the men who seemed rough
talk about Pelléas and Mélisande

the insignia on the sleeves of their black jackets:
Royal Opera House, Covent Garden

§

Two pheasants on the path near Square Wood, dumped gas canisters off the edge; the rain holds till Painter's Forstal, starts, then stops, crossing the field to the church at Ospringe.

Across the street, long dead daffodils on the roof, aerials, the grime on a wall, a sky alternating blueness and rainfall.

Someone admiring someone else's dog, or tying their shoelaces.

> Rustic Billard
> William Gladstone, Prime Minister
> Bouquet of Flowers
> Lady Motorist
> Forrester
> Basket Cutty
> Milled Rim
> Tulip Cutty
> King Edward VII Coronation
> General Gordon
> Claw
> Brontë Lady
>
> —varieties of clay pipe

§

In the beginning
space without place?

is the void uninhabitable
because there's 'no room' there?
—the first pages of Casey's book
offer enough not to continue
sheltered here from rain
a hanging basket
beneath a tree that threatens anarchy
waiting for a gap in the weather, for
holes in the sky
an avenue, or a venue

§

in the street
a strange language
(English)
            not the soft burr
of the poet I read,
my late friend,
                        something harder,
southern

§

a bird sounding like a bad clutch in a stalled car

first extensive sighting of electrified fences

Bishopsbourne—home of the hard-to-obtain Mr Jocelyn Brooke

§

Pallant Gallery, Chichester. John Craxton's 'Poet in a Landscape'. The vulgar notion of how art happens—the poet, seated on a verge, surrounded by objects of inspiration—is perhaps only a slight exaggeration, a small step from what might happen if the figure were to occupy a sofa for example, the floor strewn with books, maps, disks.

Then there's Julian Trevelyan's 'Poet escaping the Call-Up'.

But what of Blake's small frontispiece showing a naked man recoiling from a cliff while his dog plummets into the toothed jaws of a sea creature?

We are here to see Ivon Hitchens. Two rooms of his work.

He had a special liking for Belgian canvas: 'Herga', with a 'toothy' surface and hard priming, for painting with thick paint; a lighter canvas, with smoother surface, for lighter painting. The canvasses would arrive from the supplier already primed, but he would reprime them with titanium or zinc white shortly before use, as he liked to work not only on the dry white ground that gives luminosity and brilliance but also into the ground when still not quite dry so as to produce that gradation of tone which is so special to him—as is the spluttered edge of paint from a brush that is pushed into the painting rather than drawn smoothly across it.

—Peter Khoroche

the memory
of light and dark

§

The Cutty Sark on fire occasions a debate (Radio 4) on the nature of reality . . .

§

on the bridle path, behind the cemetery,
St Dunstan's,
                    then through Harbledown
(noted in Chaucer), the bells of St Nicholas

an overgrown red telephone booth

nobody uses these paths on weekdays
the sound of the A2 diminishes

'No Man's Orchard'

hazel catkins ('lamb's tails')

In Denstead Wood the track peters out completely. As a result of this confusion, reverse, then take an alternate path, blocked with rubble by Thatcherite landowners. Through South Bishop's Den to Forester's Lodge Farm, then Hitchen's Green (Hickmans) and finally, Boughton. Lunch at the White Horse.

§

Duggan's Tramps Through Kent #33
or see my *By Trailbike*
& Hot-Air Balloon Through England.

At Boughton, a truck pulled off to the side and an object *the size and apparent bulk of a man* half on the road. It is a plastic bag full of soil.

They did a lovely poem
and they practiced it
and it came out very well

unaccented vowels and unvoiced consonants

HORSE BOXES
FOR SALE

From Wingham the path crosses a field of—is it—barley? Later, after Wickhambreaux, village of suspicious people, the track is overgrown.

Descend through Hospital Wood to Fordwich 'the smallest town in England'.

§

Reading the essay on poetics (Robert Sheppard) on a warm afternoon, the street silent, birds in the backyard. Then a streetsweeper starts.

sweet singer of modernism

The scented tree (a 'pest') now out in cream flower. Hack down nondescript bush next to the shed. More and more this place resembles a ship, the prow facing the street. From here I can see through to the front windows, the black oblong of the computer before temporary curtains, angled reflections of brick in the glass.

A large bee disappears into the funnel of foxglove.

R announced unexpectedly in the pub last night that she felt 'at home' here—*here* particularly, in Faversham—whereas as much as I like it (the place, the garden &c) I don't feel that I 'belong' anywhere.

§

lupins   [drawing]   (leaves)

flax (?)   (blue flowers)

§

Nagden Marshes. Yellow patches of sky under storm clouds.
Power lines across flat fields.
The raised track divides rape from barley.

Never losing sight of Faversham's hollow steeple.

luminous blue damselflies

the 'ching', metallic call from reeds
of the 'bearded tit'

then the Swale

amid the wrack
a set of wooden stairs

§

minimalism
it's what I do

§

You pay for thinner crowds (in the British Museum), though the Enlightenment Room was as near empty as possible on a wet Sunday of a long weekend.

instruments of navigation

the 'shorthand' of early maps

Molyneux's globe anticipates the Surrealists—a huge 'Nova Gvinea' and 'Insvlae Solomones' but next to no Terra Australis.

> *Squirels which are of a grey colour*
> *we haue taken & eaten.*
> —Thomas Harriot (1590)

Also draw to life all strange birds beasts fish plants herbs trees and fruits and bring home of each sort as near as you may.
—Instructions to an artist c1582

§

An invitation to contribute to a book about The Triffids feels like the company of 'real' artists—a fragment of 'Ornithology' amid surviving members of the band and various music luminaries (Peter Blake knew he wasn't 'slumming it' designing album covers).

it's like being asked to decorate the Parthenon

§

later: Powell and Pressburger's 'A Canterbury Tale' (1944):

Their reworking
of Chaucer's epic tale, largely set in wartime Kent, centres on American army
sergeant JOHN SMITH, British soldier DENNIS PRICE and landgirl SHEILA
SIM who, before making a modern-day pilgrimage to Canterbury, solve the
bizarre mystery of a man who pours glue over the hair of village girls at night.

§

dark clouds on the weather map these last days of spring

This house, almost a model of the public / private divide. A window right
on the street where passersby and the odd curious neighbour may look
in to see me looking out at them from my computer (blinds being open).
And at the back, the walled garden accessible only to ourselves and the
birds.

the sky, at present, Baroque

a supermarket closes 79 stores in 24 hours

§

it's my birthday
I am a bear
carrying a suitcase
investigating the village

a quiet day

a fine dinner at the Gods (Goods!) Shed, then, awake at 3 am, hour of
sadness.

§

Alan Halsey's poem:
YESTERDAY THE BARRICADE
TOMORROW THE BARCODE
becomes a bookmark in the Harold
Nicholson diaries

§

Graveney Marsh,
traversed in a hurry
to get to the Sportsman

promised thunder holding off

June

the world birds inhabit
of diagonals, flipped horizons
up and down as continuum

§

Ronald Johnson's *Book of the Green Man*, a poem written over forty years
ago, takes as its anchor the seasons observed by particular authors: the
Wordsworths, Kilvert, White (Gilbert) and Palmer (Samuel), moving from
the Lakes via the Welsh Borders to Kent. Present and past interpenetrate
but there is no (1963) sense of loss, just continuity. In 2007 this sense has
evaporated.

§

travelling backwards, into the sun
for London Victoria, ultimately
the Betsy Trotwood, once home
to Subvoicive readings
and, this once, Crossing the Line
(The Plough double booked)

—tonight

✿ WYSTAN CURNOW ✿

(Ann Lauterbach 'lost her passport')—

every couple of minutes
a mobile goes off
and the person in front of me farts silently

everyone speaks Polish

(the train is delayed for fifty minutes at West Dulwich due to 'a fire on a bridge')

the sun angles into these streets

                                 (that's me)

garlic and sapphires

                         (that's someone else)

Denmark Street for instance. The ghosts of music publishers.

Ms Trotwood is there (in Farringdon Rd)
but is the reader?

                        (yes)

there's a gig downstairs
and up

so the poets read
(Peter Jaeger's poem
on hegemony
—the Canadian perspective:

N=I=X=O=N

show-
er and
tell

a b(l)ank book

rubber
dub

in the break, the bar packed

the poet smokes incessantly

Inglan
is a bitch
says L.K.J.

dozens of rollerskaters
pass down Farringdon Rd

when my mind
turns to pyrex
             (a mishearing)

In London you are never more than ten feet away from a rat.

§

a hole in a wall
leads into a garden

allotments and duck ponds
sheds and bridges

as close to willow pattern
as the Home Counties allow

light leaving the sky
the sick-bed

immersed in typography

all the books I may / may not read
or write

what would hold English matter
as 'Blue Hills' held Australian?

§

Blackbird chicks stumble through the garden with shaggy feathers and endless appetites. The opium poppies are out.

the density of woods that were bare sticks

You realise the sound of the boiler coming on downstairs is like the sound of the lift in your former residence.

§

Nor am I temperamentally suited to old age. I have no liking for dignity, sobriety, repute and authority . . . I suffer from the sad defects of every epicurean.
—Harold Nicholson

§

The problem of pattern against pattern; of describing colours on the telephone (and what did William Morris intend to hang over his wallpaper?).

§

Diagonally opposite, an elderly woman smiles as she reads the City Lights *Howl*.

§

faux
oast

§

why is there sand on the French coast
and stones on the English?

the same chalk runs beneath

rain damaged frescoes
a slight psychedelic Virgin (Boulogne)
in a boat, waves
of frozen cement

In the square of the 'new' town a market gives way to a political meeting
which in turn gives way to a wedding. Black 1940s Citröen, bonnet up,
waiting.

> *Mon oncle,*
> south of this
> out of Amiens
> an English graveyard
> 09/08/1918
> Aust^n Light Horse
> Vignacourt, some miles
> W. of Villers-Bretonneaux

out from Calais, glare and mist

does the land appear because you want it to?

false patches of light on the sea
then, dimly, Dover and the Cliffs,
a washed out strip between cloud and water,
outlines of the Castle and docks

a daguerreotype

§

> high camp
> at Quex Park
> a menagerie
> of stuffed beasts
> swinging apes
> okapi

lion and ox
in death tangle,
the lion gored
while gripping the ox
close to the heart
all this, courtesy
Major Percy
Powell-Cotton
inventor of
the diorama
his own shirt
mirrored
the ripped back
his encounter
with Leo Rex

continuous expeditions
1895–1939 (d. 1940)
adjacent, the house
crammed with Chinoiserie
he would rarely
live amidst

§

9.15, haze but no thunderclouds
as I walk west to Bysing Wood

out of Luddenham, at Poplar Hall
a cage of rottweilers howl for blood

at Uplees the sky grows heavy
an abandoned bathtub luminous in a field

but the rain holds off as I cross the Oare Marshes
remnants of explosives manufacture,

concrete bunkers,
a disused dock,

little egrets and Brent geese on the East Flood,
aura of saltmarsh

*On Sunday 2nd April 1916, 109 men and boys were killed by an explosion at the
Explosives Loading Company factory at Uplees, near Faversham. 15 tons of TNT
and 150 tons of ammonium nitrate blew up when some empty sacks caught fire
. . . [W]indows across the Thames estuary in Southend were shattered and the
tremor was felt in Norwich. The crater . . . was 40 yards across and 20 feet deep . . .
Included in the 116 dead, was the whole of the Works Fire Brigade . . . Many of
the dead were buried in a mass grave at Faversham Cemetery.*

§

The importance of strange poetry, of unfamiliarity.

a mind always elsewhere
not focussed on text
but allowing it to shift
as a film before perception
odd detail in clefts
part of the net seen clear
the weave otherwise vague

§

the two rivers, Thames and Medway,
refuse to mingle their exhalations
—the Medway brown and white,
the Thames green

*The Medway has a concealed delta, infiltrating both Grain and the orchard
landscape south of Sheppey. That is why Sittingbourne and Faversham and a
whole band of villages and hamlets . . . are exactly where they are, waterside*

places where no creek is suspected and seemingly owing nothing to the Medway direct. Ocean boats have been built here, timber stored and seasoned, explosives manufactured and fine antique papers laid—all in an area where a coarse map or plain common sense would suggest people's main concern should be lowland sheep and then apples.

—Michael Baldwin

§

A day on the South Downs:

The church in Berwick, St Michael (of which Lee wrote), its murals by Duncan Grant, Vanessa Bell and Quentin by turns wooden and radiant, the church at the end of a lane.

The house and garden of Charleston, the austerity of the interior (you know what Auden meant when he desired above all else modern plumbing).

Statuary in the gardens by those who play at Gods.

Then Firle, staid, half-finished in its grandeur.
The 'long' (not the 'short') view.

so what's *heimlich*? old money
heating its cavernous ante-rooms?
a sense of order outside which
is chaos ('industry')?

§

Approaching the University, all haze blown away, floating clouds above a semi-rural prospect, spires, aspirations.

what do I do

after this?

135

enact *the*

return to lyric?

(notes from
the Gulbenkian, my Armenian
alma mater)

a hand appears
on frosted glass behind the image of
a clock face

it is 5.50 pm,
June 18th, 2007,

year of nothing in particular

why do we
so often choke
on our own spittle?

Chariots of Fire
meets Rocky
meets Shine
—on wheels!

(a short history
of recent cinema)

did Virginia Woolf like the Marx Brothers?

§

A chubby schoolboy wearing a shirt that makes him look like Brian
Wilson circa 1963 describes a film script with a 'brilliant' ending (death).
His replacement in the carriage phones someone for £200 to replace
what she'd given to a boyfriend who otherwise would 'have his legs cut
off'.

Blundered upon: the house of Dante Gabriel Rossetti (1851), subsequently William Morris and Edward Burne-Jones (1856–9), Red Lion Square.

§

The Crab and Winkle Way ran from 1830 to 1932 as a passenger service, then till 1952 as a goods line. The present bicycle path opened in 1999. Halfway, a pond, the site of a winching station (to haul the trains up the slope from Canterbury).

§

a nail (hand-fashioned)
a feather
a blue egg

§

All over Westminster neophytes are falling over themselves.

—Giles Fraser

§

I understand the profusion of Palmer, that seasonal eruption that sinks back into the earth (though Pam sends photos of Blackheath under snow—more snow than we'd get here).

§

rain
a window seat

ancient music

§

at Willesden Green I duck non-existent beams
in an Edwardian house where
an upstairs neighbour is locked out, barefoot

enquire after the floods up north

with age, how much
prior life is rehearsed?

though it seems new
with a new audience

small press books from the seventies and eighties
the wonders of possibility

could I do this myself? now?
an edition of, what?

§

'How well I understand Rimbaud', [Valentine Penrose] said, 'and his hatred
of perfection. That is what is the matter here',—she indicated the room with
a vague gesture—'all these pictures. I should like to take a piece of chalk and
scribble on them all!'

—David Gascoyne

after the thorough spring-cleaning and scouring I went through last winter . . . I
now know what I am going to do and what I am. Approximately.

§

Herne Bay to Whitstable,

a man in military camouflage
talking to himself

danger: barbed wire mesh resurfacing
near Swalecliffe—from the war?

trails in the sky

the bad weather
happens elsewhere
(Sheffield in flood)

telephone booths under water

—these images seem Australian (or American) in their scale—

in Faberland clouds are fluffy briefcases
the rain falls like documents

in Gippsland, floods,
Bairnsdale, Stratford, Sale, Traralgon, Lakes Entrance

Raymond Island evacuated
the Imperial Hotel under water (again)

dams 20% full now overflow

you can't tell the river from the fields

July

at Dungeness, all is aftermath, dropped on pebbles
as habitation, industry, trash.
to mark any part of this 'private'
is senseless, over it
the nuclear plant (its own planet)
secured on a flood plain

if art can be made of old rope
shoes and driftwood
what follows?

everything here is deposited
everything can be carried off

§

at Great Dixter
a house
altered
disembowelled
eviscerated
put back together
by Lutyens

the great hall
formerly dirt floor
and smoke-hole,
later, high table

and now, postcards,
books by the late owner, the gardener

§

days of rain, thunder
in the afternoon, the glass
falling by the hour

housebound (except
for the Post Office queue

nothing to do
but WORK (!,
the Maynard G
Krebs exclamation)

§

Independence Day
indoors, *the wettest*
June since 1912

the street seems dead quiet at 6 pm,
Elvis (and Three Dog Night)
in The Sun, then
what seems to be the soundtrack
of a silent film the bar fills to,
heavy furniture shifted upstairs, *nothing*
like thunder

you can almost hear the rain coming
(they should play Ann Peebles)

south, the sky
darkens again, the garden
left to myriad sparrows,
the spuggies almost
fledged, bathe
in dust under
the cotoneaster

one mysterious plant appears to be a potato,
another, with white flowers at the top
of long-leaved stems is, what?

a scraping in the walls and timbers
—the famous London rat within
its ten foot radius?

the neighbour gutter, uncapped,
overflows
on the dog rose

these dog days

§

sunlight in the garden

blades of some late summer plant

In 1967 I saved my pocket money to buy the *Collected Poems* of Louis MacNeice, a poet I'd discovered for myself in Robin Skelton's Penguin anthology *Poetry of the Thirties*. I'd not taken to Auden or the other two horsemen though the English surrealists—Gascoyne, Roger Roughton, Hugh Sykes Davies—had intrigued me. I didn't imagine that Davies was a classicist or worked for the BBC.

§

One of the things I very much wanted to record a short description of here, was the exhilarating beauty of the Kentish landscape, between Tunbridge and Sevenoaks, as I saw it just then, on one of the earliest days in Spring, this year. (I had just been reading the Samuel Palmer book I mentioned a few pages back, and I think this must have had a certain influence on the way I saw the scenery of Kent that morning: everything painted itself on my sight with the vivid intensity of a rare vision; and the countryside before my eyes happened to be the very same as that in which Palmer lived in his youth and where he produced the

best and most personal of his early work.)
—David Gascoyne 30.IV.42

§

☞   Cooting Blodden

> a trig point, from which
> view storm over east coast
> the outline of Richborough power station (disused)

the weird thing about Patrixbourne—no pubs

§

France, through the tunnel.

Montreuil, a hill town,

though *'sur mer'* seems imprecise at best.

The sand blown toward the French coast by

prevailing wind.

La Manche—the sleeve
preferable to 'English'
for the Channel

§

I have become a relentless empiricist. But empiricism carried to an
extreme becomes a kind of religion—a theology at least—where
everything (the impossible!) must be included. As, on my grandfather's
orders, my uncle counted and positioned stones in a driveway.

an empiricist, and a minimalist, for whom
texts strip down to phrases of music
and art is a way of passing time

Remember that critic who suggested that my work was 'the poetry of lists' (I don't think she meant this to be flattering)? There's a philosophy that assumes all things are lists, or made up of them.

little contingencies
for whose delight?

not the brashly confident young barman?

Are the poems charms against death? As though to keep singing (as the birds) denoted existential terror.

bizarrely, the pub's soundtrack is Iron Butterfly: 'In a gadda da vida'

§

Stour Valley Walk:

telephoto lenses
head for the hides

        in Stodmarsh village
        poultry in the street

        then mud and
        'bull in field'

            to Fordwich

chill in the beer garden, small pellets of rain on the Stour
(will I walk to Canterbury or take a bus?)

                 . . . walk
(don't run, 64)

        the threat of sunlight

traverse stubble
(an *Ear in a Wheatfield?*)

      small
      white   (or yellow)
      quatre-
      foil

      avoid
      golf
      balls

then heavy undergrowth,
two jogging soldiers

they seemed like some curious variant of the human species—Homo Sapiens,
var. militaris

            struggle through to the bike path

WARNING
troops training

another sign,
illegible

—I've taken the wrong turn—

the second sign reads:

WARNING
do not touch suspicious objects
—they may explode and kill you

walk through Canterbury Army Barracks
past a sentry with submachine gun
and a further sign:

HEIGHTENED ALERT

no joke!

'Soon he was tucked in his bed with a cup of hot cocoa'

§

A Victorian print: 'Amateur Hop-Picking in Kent'. Finely dressed ladies at amusement, an example of the upper caste playing at labour (imagine *having* to work). Instead, things simply appear, as they do for us.

§

everyone I love
gathered in

(or gathering in)

the ratty staple-jobs,
the screenprints, now
acid-free paper

outside, the vegetation encroaches,
everything needs cutting back

do we?

§

so, the scattering
of phrases, the mulch
making up this (or
making this up), things
don't hold until
a strange discourse
takes over, the notes

blind to purpose
except the track of
improbability, in fear
of taking up too much
of the page (*off*
the page? no,
Mister O, *on* it
firmly

the distant embarrassment
of 'my government' (this
should be pronounced
in *patois*)
Pam's
trans-global reference
—people to see in Potsdam
(*things to do* . . .)

though first I have
to write my review

§

Thunder at 5 am clears later to warm and humid. Drive southwest. At Bateman's, Kipling's gigantic Rolls Royce, tyres almost tractor-size. Back roads to Bodiam, thence Rye. James' garden shed destroyed by bombs. The house of Paul Nash.

St Swithin's Day

§

I wrote somewhere about the chronicle, compared to the 'history', noting rather than shaping. But noting *is* shaping and shaping is shaping *shapes*.

§

age that turns
all our brightness
to stone, the riffs
a decade old, that
grim flower
a torrent down
the street

I journeyed down the central path, the path
of the obvious that leads through the
obvious only to the obvious.

                        —Steve Kelen

§

roses
unfurl

rain
blows up
from France

Ivy Cottage
opposite Bishopsbourne Forge
(the NT sign
obscured)

in private woodland,
the tower:

MARGATE CORPORATION

DISTRICT WATER WORKS

1903

From the village, the watertower was invisible: hidden from our sight by the
high chalky plateau of Barham downs . . . It was a landmark, and also a limit:

bounding in that north-easterly direction, the familiar zone covered by our afternoon walks . . .

It was an extraordinary structure: not 'functional' at all . . . but built with the solidity . . . of a stockbroker's villa in Surrey . . . Four columns of brick-work, converging at their summits, formed four corresponding arches: the tower had the look of an arcade or a viaduct folded in upon itself to form a quadrilateral . . .

It was the pioneer-period of Kent coal: in a few more years, it was commonly predicted, East Kent would become Black Country. It never did; the few collieries which were developed remained localized, remote and . . . unsuspected.

—Jocelyn Brooke

§

approaching London
the semicircle of cloud (a regular formation
presaging what?

nothing apparently,
African music on Warren Street:
The Brotherhood of Breath, 1972

crossed town to Coram's Fields and Lambs Conduit
(did not meet William Blake)
but passed, accidentally, through gardens (St George's),
a gold statue:
Flora?
ankle deep in primulas

§

you grasp a piece of conversation
hang on after the moment has passed
as though it were an object not a process

yet your writing has never done this

§

cut flowers, a marble vase on the sill,

outside / inside

for David Jones it could be
all of Wales

the M5 under water, the M4 blocked by slippages

a water-rat
nosing across the creek
downstream from the old mill

§§§

Berlin

Miss the flight by ten minutes. Travel back slowly to Faversham. Will the neighbours think I'm a burglar, crashing round at 11.30, taking the frozen milk out of the refrigerator? I will wear something from my suitcase (which will make it lighter).

When I should have been on the U-Bahn I was on a slow train through Meopham.

suits *and* backpacks
the neue korporatism

§

A day later I make it, at least to the Metro Bar, Gatwick. At the adjoining table two men drink respectively a third and two-thirds of Guinness. The flight to Accra is postponed indefinitely, a piece of metal found in the engine. Bags, inaccessible, already on the plane. And *my* flight delayed 45 minutes. The sense of England on holiday as a form of punishment.

Austerity Britain, £3.00 off.

over Berlin, Elsheimer's moon!

thank you for travelling easyJet anyway . . . now you can disembark, really

§

Auguststraße   rain

to venture into the streets

with the purpose of Sartre's waiter. I am 'being a tourist' as I walk down to Unter den Linden and along to the Brandenburg Gate. Then I walk back, the same route.

einbahnstraße (!)

the rain is fine and constant

כל-בו
KOLBO
bagel bakery

ich hütte die rechnung

§

Afternoon at the Wall museum in Bernauerstraße, site of the fallen church (1985). A film shows people evacuated from the wall-zone. A couple carry a doll's house down the street. The wall intersected with houses (windows bricked up). The familiarity of sentry-boxes less than twenty years ago.

§

The Alte Nationalgalerie. Böcklin's self-portrait is good, but most of his other work ('Island of the Dead' missing) is disappointing. Even Caspar David Friedrich doesn't look all that great ('Woman at a window' is interesting—the figure seems to have no substance; something not apparent in reproduction). The German 'Impressionists' however are, against expectation, good. It's art that tends to be ignored in the modernist framework because it is several years 'behind' the French.

In the Pergamon Museum we run out of wind. Swathes of objects moved in bulk from Greece and the Middle-East.

Berliner Galerie. Emilio Vedova: 'Absurde Berliner Tagebuch '64' (walk, don't run).

I began work . . . with 15 little gas fires(!): in January in Berlin . . . on the look out for plywood in the warehouses on the embankments of the Spree; wire and rope in Spandau—, in the area of the Karl-Marx-Straße, in the direction of the "wall", the hinges . . .

BUT!! My Berlin plurimi: They have the dizziness of a large, unknown space, hostile, a terrible challenge to endure, inevitable *. . . An absurd challenge!*

—Vedova

in the holocaust tower
a tight corner, light
slim, from above, sounds
from the street, tears

DADA KEBABS

or (Otto Dix Restaurant):

jacket potato with herbal quark

August

Sensory overload at Schloss Charlottenburg, in particular the porcelain room and the chapel. A partly stuffed deer hangs from the edge of a painted ceiling. Lightness in the oval rooms overlooking the garden; heaviness elsewhere. A dining table laden with sauce boats.

Nebelkrähe—a brown and black bird

in the Bambi Bar, 'the dark stuff'
(not what Nick Kent meant, but *dunkles weisen*)

§

The Stasi Museum,
fake logs, hinged,
recording apparatus inside,
stones with tiny lens holes

poetry especially is suspect

a room full of body-odour samples

Imagine someone photographing this notebook, its mash of inconsequential politics, aesthetic prejudice, household junk.

'from the currywurst stall they went to the kebab shop'

Strangest of all, the experience of taking photographs in the Stasi headquarters. Desks and tape recorders marooned in the early 1970s. The complex itself is a musty piece of 1960s architecture with a latticed concrete screen before the entrance. The landscape around it consists of acres of tower blocks. This is not the kind of office one would associate with dictators like Ceaucescu. It is modest, banal . . . a tea room with three-plate electric stove, an ordinary bathroom.

Communism was already a lost ideal by the time the DDR was formed.

Railway stations on the way to nowhere (the Nordbahnhof). The Wall, grey on one side, coloured the other.

§

mauerkunst:

Helmut Newton's model, 1963, an old newspaper photograph with the unclear outline of the figure corrected by hand. The model holds a pair of field-glasses, back turned to us, atop wooden steps, looking across the Wall through barbed wire.

Kruckenberg and Witt's sleeping Venus (after Giorgione) before the Wall, 1972.

A section wallpapered with 1960s furniture foreground.

CHILDREN OF PARADISE. PIG wurzer. Schade, das Beton nicht brennt. ASPHALT NACHT. Sofortige Öffnung der Drupa-Jugendsgruppe. MAUER VERRECKE. **Guerre froide.** EGGS UND HOPP. MILLIONS OF DEAD COPS. Axel und Christian waren hier 14.10.82. The WALL must broke. PUNK DUNK ÜBER ALLED I LOVE IT. **FUCK THE SYSTEM. BREAK DOWN THE WALL. FUCK THE WALL.** Das ist die letze Hoffnung. E PROIBIDO PRIBIR. Nichts Neues aus Ost und West. Weg mit diesem Monstrum. DINGO FENCE MATERIAL JIM DALE THANKS TO DFFB. JE TE SURVEILLE TENDRE—MENT DE LOIN. 5 min. Punk sets you free. Mauerstadt.

—Bohlau Verlag, 2007

The area between walls was razed for vision (the church across Bernauerstraße demolished as late as 1985).

it's just around the corner
from Brecht's house

[end of Berlin segment]

§§§

Documents on the sale of 15 West Street date back to the eighteenth century with a will from 1738, some years before the house was built, and up to 1960. In the early 1940s the bakery caught fire; this (the backyard shed) dating back probably to the early twentieth century.

the back garden, overgrown
in the space of a week

out of Faversham
a stone chapel
—flint, worked over
Roman brick

a series of false-starts

§

Whitstable,
figures on a stony beach

(beer from the Neptune in plastic cups)

a mauve twilight over Sheppey
                    —earlier, the town's
parade, end of the Oyster Festival,
                              beauty queens
from neighbour villages,
                    a fife band,
bored children with pompoms

a strange air of the 1940s (or earlier)
caught on digital cameras—

barbecues between the groynes

later that night
a hedgehog in the lane

finally, the heat

§

It's almost a year since I walked in Church Wood. Again I get lost. What appear on the ordnance map to be foot tracks, bridle paths and unsurfaced roads appear on the ground interchangeable. Entering the woods at Upper Harbledown and intending to emerge at Blean I end up somehow on the Denstroude Road and have to cut back to the Whitstable Road at Red Lion House. After this everything relates to the map again.

traffic, or
wind through pines?

summer's cauldron

the rowan berries (?) are out,
probably poisonous, and sloe,
safe but inedible

after Honey Hill, a feast
(the phenomenon, strange for me, of being able to eat
blackberries from the hedge
(in Australia they would probably have been sprayed with
herbicide).

out from Clowes Farm
the harvest is over

§

forced growth coming to stasis
things here have extended as far as they will
(in February the yard was under snow, if only for a day)

laughter in a beer garden doors up
a blackbird flexes its wings

still, the minute
tokens of procreation

feathered seeds, rosehips,
webs arrayed like nets

                              the thrush,
always something in its beak, legs splayed
on the rim of a garden pot

cracks its foodstuff
against concrete and vanishes

light hangs in the sky,
gulls against cirrus

a light breeze
stirs the petals

pour into a large glass
in one smooth action

§

'Elderly Frightened by Yobs', reads a local billboard. The 'yobs', I guess,
denizens of The Swan (a half-hour of 'anti-social behaviour' after Friday
closing time).

§

the gnats 'wail'
pas de deux
blackbird and thrush

'goose bumps'

beaks scratching the guttering,
manic at dusk

        tomorrow's storm brews
        over the Shipwright,

        over duckboards and clinkers,
        the high-tension lines

        banking toward Whitstable

        the wind will probably
        lift these plastic tables tomorrow

        . . . or tonight

        on a mown lawn, in a ditch
        beneath the dyke

        weather bearing up
        from Sussex

        —will I be wet
        by Faversham Creek?—

        my office
        in various places

        where this
        gets written

        the rumble of an airliner
        above these clouds

        this country

a toy giraffe
abandoned in the garden

across the marsh
a wind farm, white

under broken cloud

the black sail
of a yawl

a large blue heron
risen from the reed beds

Rain and strengthening winds, but a kind of holding-back as though preparing for worse to come. The papers forecast an early end to summer this year, unlike last, when it hung on through September.

§

driving north, storm cloud to the west

Corby: the origins of the American flag: a window in the church

York: the Treasurer's House, remodelled by Frank Green. In the kitchen Rosemary asks the volunteer what constitutes 'mock turtle soup'. He says 'turtles' until his attention is drawn to the qualifier. Then he's nonplussed.

cathedral towns   junk food

And more rain, Lindesfarne, Alnwick, Newcastle (swallows). Wet streets down to the Tyne. Smokers standing in the rain outside the pubs. The old bridge near the hotel has been boarded up for three years. The window of the restaurant is wide-screen, lights, cops, a soundtrack, a voice-over. Men who plainly aren't gay in outfits someone dared them to wear. Women in skimpy shorts and police ties.

The Baltic: the problem of art that is fundamentally conceptual but that insists on illustrating itself (the practice often painstaking and literal).

difference and repetition
(two f's and two t's)
Tyne and Tees?

'Gonna Take You Back to Walker' (the Animals)
—it's only two miles out of town

and where is
Morden Tower?

a clear day seems somehow miraculous

Schwitters 'Merzbarn', transported from the Lakes District by Richard Hamilton (1965), reassembled in the Hatton Gallery.

We leave 'understated elegance' and 'relaxed dining' (the opposite is unthinkable), driving south and west for Earl Sterndale and Matlock Bath over the Howden Moors and Bleaklow Uplands around Kinder Scout to the limestone edge on the Dove just opposite the Packhorse at Crowdecote and back by Glutton Bridge.

breakfast, under the Heights of Abraham

is the trouser-press
an English institution?

north, then south east,
mist across the Fens

in King's Lynn
sleetish rain

next day, via Swaffham,
a fake Iceni village,
a church with collapsed round tower

rain increasing,
the flint mines at Grime's Graves

endless roundabouts

§

A mirror falls off the wall upstairs. Smoke
in a long disused fireplace

fire in Greece
flood in Queensland
a hole in the universe, southeast of Orion,
six billion light years across

two men in North Wales, fined
for selling woodland bluebells

a glass hip-flask
which belonged to the poet Robert Burns

§

Basil Bunting wisely aspired to *minor poet / not conspicuously dishonest.* An
honorary 'southron', I don't have too much choice.

I have a language to learn.

§

later:

22 across . . .

'Bill Fagen . . .'

        four down . . .

                'traders'

18 down:

      'Disney characters'

           'is Peter one of the lost boys from Hook?'

five down, 'retreated'

          'backed off . . .
          surrendered . . .'

    17 across . . .
    'embellishments'

§

stillness and mildness
presaging autumn?

red trellis
over darker brick

scraped timbers

layers, like
A Furnace

a smudged page
submerged

out the window
bright berries

listen to Little Barrie

§

burnt umber on black, shapes dissolved
for which the best light is half-light,
illuminating but not reflective

a painting you can always almost see
—this on the side wall of a long room,
its far end, odd-shaped panes, sunlit,
a parallelogram on the carpet

coloured glass bottles
                            the pattern
subsuming everything, unrolled
as a rug, but endless
                            fading soon enough
as though a season were accomplished in moments

how much of it 'adds up'?

a buzzing insect enters then leaves the room

CPSIA information can be obtained at www.ICGtesting.com
Printed in the USA
BVOW07s0027301014

372887BV00001B/207/P